An Empirical Study of the Effects of *Ex Ante* Licensing Disclosure Policies on the Development of Voluntary Technical Standards

by

Jorge L. Contreras
American University
Washington College of Law
Washington, DC

for

**National Institute of
Standards and Technology**
U.S. Department of Commerce

NIST Standards Services Group
Under NIST Contract No. SB134110SE1033

This publication was produced as part of contract SB134110SE1033
with the National Institute of Standards and Technology. The contents of this
publication do not necessarily reflect the views or policies of the National
Institute of Standards and Technology or the U.S. Government.

GCR 11-934
Release Date: June 27, 2011

An Empirical Study of the Effects of *Ex Ante* Licensing Disclosure Policies on the Development of Voluntary Technical Standards

Jorge L. Contreras

Table of Contents

Acknowledgements

This study was funded by the U.S. National Institute of Standards and Technology (NIST) under Contract No. SB134110SE1033. The author gratefully acknowledges the guidance and support of NIST staff.

This study could not have been completed without the able assistance of Dr. Melody Goodman (statistical analysis) and Yen-Shyang Tseng (research assistance) at Washington University in St. Louis.

Many thanks are also due to Ray Alderman and John Rynearson of VITA and David Ringle of IEEE, who provided invaluable information and insight relating to their organizations.

The author also thanks the following for their valuable comments, suggestions and insights: James Gibson, Kimberly Kaphingst, John Kulick, Michael Lindsay, Steve Mills, Gil Ohana, Scott Peterson, Robert Skitol, Tim Simcoe, Claudia Tapia Garcia, and the participants in the 2011 Arizona State University Conference on Technology Standards in a Globalized World and the Federal Trade Commission's 2011 Workshop on Intellectual Property Rights in Standard Setting: Tools to Prevent Patent Hold-Up.

Statement of Interests

The author serves a legal consultant to the Internet Engineering Task Force (IETF), one of the organizations discussed in this report. No consideration was received from IETF in connection with this report or study.

I.   Executive Summary

The threat of patent "hold-up", in which patent holders demand compensation from implementers of technical standards following wide-scale adoption of those standards, has focused significant governmental, academic and industry attention on means for averting such scenarios. One method of addressing patent hold-up risk is the imposition of an obligation on patent holders participating in the standardization process to license their standards-essential patents to implementers on "fair, reasonable and nondiscriminatory" (FRAND) terms. The precise meaning of FRAND commitments, however, have proven difficult to determine with precision, leading to further litigation and uncertainty. An alternative approach proposes that each patent holder participating in a standards-development organization (SDO) to disclose in advance ("*ex ante*") the material terms on which it will license its standards-essential patents. The risks and merits of such *ex ante* licensing disclosure policies have been debated extensively. In 2006-07 the U.S. Department of Justice approved limited *ex ante* licensing disclosure policies adopted by two U.S.-based voluntary SDOs, VMEBus International Trade Association (VITA) and the Institute for Electrical and Electronics Engineers (IEEE). At the time these policies were adopted, critics predicted that early disclosure of patent licensing terms could lead to anticompetitive conduct by standards implementers and would unduly burden the already lengthy and costly standards development process.

This study represents the first empirical investigation of the effects of *ex ante* licensing disclosure policies on standards development. We examined data relating to SDO membership, standards projects initiated, standards approved, speed of the standardization process, individual time commitment and quality of standards for VITA, IEEE and the Internet Engineering Task Force (IETF) from 2003/4 to 2010. We also conducted a survey of VITA participants to assess individual reactions to the adoption of the VITA *ex ante* policy in 2007.

In general, we did not find that *ex ante* disclosure policies resulted in measurable negative effects on the number of standards started or adopted, personal time commitments or quality of standards, nor was there compelling evidence that *ex ante* policies caused the lengthening of time required for standardization or the depression of royalty rates. There was some evidence to suggest that the adoption of *ex ante* policies may have contributed positively to some of these variables. Moreover, a significant majority of VITA participants responding to our survey felt that the information elicited by the organization's *ex ante* policy was important and improved the overall openness and transparency of the standards-development process. Thus, while there are numerous areas in which further study and analysis may be warranted, and other organizations in which the implementation of *ex ante* policies may have different effects, we conclude, on the basis of the data that we have reviewed, that the process-based criticisms of *ex ante* policies and the predicted negative effects flowing from the adoption of such polices, are not supported by the evidence reviewed.

II.   Background

A.   Development of Voluntary Technical Standards. Technical standards are detailed sets of instructions, specifications or protocols that must be complied with in order to achieve a particular technical purpose. Depending on the standard, this purpose may be to achieve a minimum level of safety (e.g., security of automobile seatbelts), a desired environmental effect (e.g., reduction of carbon emissions), or interoperability among products and technologies sold by different vendors (e.g., TCP/IP, USB, WiFi, GSM and other computing, networking and telecommunications standards). This last category of standards, those that are intended to promote technological interoperability and which are prevalent in the so-called information, communications and technology (ICT) sector, are generally voluntary, in that compliance is not mandated by any governmental or regulatory body. Rather, market participants elect to comply with voluntary interoperability standards to make their products and technologies competitive in a networked, interdependent marketplace.[1]

Voluntary interoperability standards are developed within a variety of organizational structures including treaty organizations such as the International Organization for Standardization (ISO) and International Telecommunications Union (ITU), regional standards developing organizations such as the European Telecommunications Standards Institute (ETSI), professional and technical organizations such as the Institute of Electrical and Electronics Engineers (IEEE) and the VMEBus International Trade Association (VITA), and less formalized consortia such as the Internet Engineering Task Force (IETF) and Worldwide Web Consortium (W3C).[2] In the United States, the American National Standards Institute (ANSI) acts both as the accreditation body for SDOs that wish to develop American National Standards,[3] as well as the United States representative to ISO and other international bodies.

B.   Patent Hold-Up in Standards-Setting. SDOs typically hold no patent rights in the standards developed by their members. Rather, participants in the standards development process (whether companies or individuals) retain their ownership of standardized technology and may obtain patents that claim implementations of these standards.[4] This ability to patent standardized technology is perceived to lead to a risk of patent "hold-up", meaning that a participant in the standards development process may guide a standard toward its own patent position, or may subsequently seek patent protection over

---

[1] *See, e.g.* CARL SHAPIRO & HAL R. VARIAN, INFORMATION RULES: A STRATEGIC GUIDE TO THE NETWORK ECONOMY 245-48 (1999).

[2] A more detailed description of the multifaceted standards development "ecosystem" can be found in Intellectual Property Owners Association, Standards Primer – An Overview of the Standards Setting Bodies and Patent-Related Issues That Arise in the Context of Standards-Setting Activities (Sept. 2009) (available   at http://www.ipo.org/AM/Template.cfm?Section=Patents&Template=/MembersOnly.cfm&NavMenuID=1454&ContentID=24139&DirectListComboInd=D).

[3] There are currently approximately 220 ANSI-accredited SDOs.

[4] This study does not address copyrights in standards documents, an issue that has also proven contentious in recent years.

aspects of the standardized technology, and then seek to extract unanticipated royalty payments from other implementers of the standard after the standard is widely adopted or "locked-in".[5] The legal and economics literature frequently cite patent hold-up in the standards-setting context as having negative implications, both for individual market participants and the market as a whole.[6]

C.   *SDO Patent Policies.* In order to avoid hold-up situations, and in response to several high profile instances of alleged patent hold-up in the standards-setting context,[7] many SDOs have implemented formal policies designed to alleviate the perceived risks of patent hold-up. These policies fall into two general categories: disclosure policies and licensing policies, and often include elements of both. Disclosure policies typically require participants in the standards development process to disclose patents they hold that would necessarily be infringed by an implementation of the standard (typically referred to as "essential" patents).[8] Licensing policies typically require that participants grant implementers licenses under their essential patents on terms that are "reasonable and non-discriminatory" (RAND) or "fair, reasonable and non-discriminatory" (FRAND).[9]

D.   *FRAND Licensing Requirements.* As noted above, many SDO licensing policies require that patent holders grant licenses to implementers of their standards on FRAND terms. But despite the intuitive appeal of this designation, a consistent and practical definition of FRAND has proven notoriously difficult to define with precision.[10] In several recent cases parties have disputed whether the terms under which licenses have been offered violate or conform with FRAND requirements:

> *Nokia v. Qualcomm* (Del. Chancery 2007): Nokia alleged that Qualcomm failed to offer FRAND licensing terms in violation of its obligations to ETSI.

---

[5] *See* U.S. Federal Trade Commission, The Evolving IP Marketplace: Aligning Patent Notice and Remedies with Competition at 191 (2011) (hereinafter "FTC 2011 Report") and HAL R. VARIAN, JOSEPH FARRELL & CARL SHAPIRO, THE ECONOMICS OF INFORMATION TECHNOLOGY – AN INTRODUCTION 81 (2004).

[6] *See, e.g.,* Mark A. Lemley, *Ten Things to do About Patent Holdup of Standards (and One Not To),* 48 BOSTON COLL. L. REV. 149, 150-52 (2007), Mark Lemley & Carl Shapiro, *Patent Holdup and Royalty Stacking,* 85 TEX. L. REV. 1991 (2007), Robert A. Skitol, *Concerted Buying Power: Its Potential For Addressing The Patent Holdup Problem in Standard Setting,* 72 ANTITRUST L.J. 727, 729-30 (2005).

[7] *See, e.g., In re. Dell Computer Corp.,* 121 F.T.C. 616 (1996), *Rambus, Inc. v. Infineon Technologies AG,* 318 F.3d 1081 (Fed. Cir. 2003), cert. denied, 124 S.Ct. 227 (2003).

[8] *See, generally,* AMERICAN BAR ASSOCIATION, COMMITTEE ON TECHNICAL STANDARDIZATION, SECTION OF SCIENCE & TECHNOLOGY LAW, STANDARDS DEVELOPMENT PATENT POLICY MANUAL (Jorge L. Contreras, ed., 2007) (hereinafter "ABA MANUAL").

[9] *See, generally,* ABA Manual, *supra* note 8, at 56-67. Commentators have been unable to agree on any substantive difference between RAND and FRAND commitments. Thus, for the sake of expediency, the term FRAND will be used throughout this paper.

[10] *See, e.g.,* SHAPIRO & VARIAN, *supra* note 1, at 241, Andrew Updegrove, *Ex Ante Disclosure: Risks, Rewards, Process and Alternatives,* CONSORTIUM STANDARDS BUL., June 2006, 1, 4-5; Anne Layne-Farrar, A. Jorge Padilla & Richard Schmalensee, Pricing Patents for Licensing in Standard-Setting Organizations: Making Sense of FRAND Commitments, 74 ANTITRUST L.J. 671, 671-72 (2007); Marc Rysman & Tim Simcoe, *A NAASTy Alternative to RAND Pricing Commitments* at 2 (working paper 2011) (available at http://people.bu.edu/tsimcoe/documents/published/NAAST.pdf).

Apple v. Nokia (D. Del. 2009): Apple argued that Nokia's royalty and grantback requirements violated ETSI and IEEE FRAND commitments.

CUT FATT (FCC 2009): Digital television manufacturers petitioned U.S. Federal Communications Commission to rule that Funai's 5% royalty on a digital television patent violated the FCC's FRAND requirement for the ATSC standard.

Zoran v. DTS (N.D. Cal. 2009): Zoran sued DTS, a fellow member of the Blu-ray Disc Association, for alleged non-compliance with FRAND licensing obligations.

Microsoft v. Motorola (W.D. Wash. 2010) Microsoft alleged that Motorola failed to comply with IEEE's FRAND requirements for licensing patents covering the WLAN and H.264 standards.

These cases represent a recent and growing trend to dispute the meaning of "FRAND", particularly with regard to royalty levels, in the standards development context.

FRAND licensing commitments can lead to disputes because there is no generally-accepted, objective standard by which "reasonableness" (or "nondiscrimination") can be measured. In order to make a FRAND determination, the specific facts of each situation must be evaluated.[11] These facts include not only relevant market norms for royalties, but also customary practices relating to non-royalty terms such as reciprocity, grantbacks, defensive suspension, confidentiality and the like. Also, given that a patent holder's FRAND licensing terms are often not revealed until negotiations occurring *after* a standard has been adopted (i.e., "locked-in"), parties involved in standards setting can experience uncertainty regarding the ultimate cost of adopting a standard encumbered by patents. Moreover, after lock-in of a standard, the patent holder's leverage in any negotiation increases enormously.[12] Put another way, FRAND licensing commitments may be said to do no more than substitute the risk of hold-up arising from unknown *patents* with hold-up arising from unknown *licensing* terms.

E.   Ex Ante *Disclosure of Licensing Terms as a Proposed Solution.* Several commentators have suggested that hold-up issues may be alleviated by requiring patent holders to disclose the royalty rates and material licensing terms on which they are willing to license essential patents *prior to* the approval of the standard (i.e., before the

---

[11] In this regard, commentators have pointed to the 15 *Georgia-Pacific* factors used in assessing "reasonable" royalty rates for patent damages calculations. *See, e.g.*, Michele K. Herman, *How the Deal is Done, Part 1*, LANDSLIDE, Sept/Oct 2010, 35, 37 (citing Georgia-Pacific Corp. v. U.S. Plywood Corp., 318 F. Supp 1116 (S.D.N.Y. 1970)). Nevertheless, the *Georgia-Pacific* factors themselves have been criticized as imprecise and indeterminate, and a full discussion of the calculation of patent damages is beyond the scope of this report.

[12] SHAPIRO & VARIAN, *supra* note 1, at 136-41.

fact or "*ex ante*").[13] According to this theory, such an *ex ante* licensing disclosure policy[14] would prevent patent holders from demanding unexpectedly high royalties (subject only to the ambiguous FRAND requirement) after a standard has been adopted and locked-in. Advance disclosure of royalty rates, it is argued, would enable SDO participants to evaluate the cost of including particular patented technologies in a standard *prior* to adoption, and would thus enable more efficient decision making with respect to the technical design of the standard. That is, if a patent holder disclosed a royalty rate that was exorbitant, or multiple patent holders disclosed royalty rates that, in the aggregate, could not be supported by projected profits from the sale of products implementing the standard, then standards-developers could theoretically adjust the design of the standard to avoid one or more of these patents and/or opt for an alternative technology covered by fewer or no such patents early in the process.[15]

F. Criticisms of Ex Ante Proposals.

1.   *Legal Criticisms.* Critics argue that *ex ante* policies will impede standards-setting processes and create additional legal risks for participants. The most commonly-asserted *legal* objections to *ex ante* policies center around antitrust concerns. For example, it has been suggested that *ex ante* licensing negotiations could facilitate the improper exchange of information among competitors (i.e., multiple competing patent

---

[13] Lemley, *supra* note 6, at 158-59, Gil Ohana, Marc Hansen & Omar Shah, *Disclosure and Negotiation of Licensing Terms Prior to Adoption of Industry Standards: Preventing Another Patent Ambush?* [2003] EUROPEAN COMPETITION L. REV. 644, 648-50 (2003), Skitol, *supra* note 6, at 741-42.

[14] In this report, the term "*ex ante* policy" is used to designate an SDO patent policy requiring or permitting disclosure of licensing terms for patents essential to implementation of a standard prior to approval of the final standard. This nomenclature can be confusing to the uninitiated, as a large number of SDO intellectual property policies require disclosure of *patents* essential to the implementation of a standard prior to approval, but do not require (or expressly permit) disclosure of *licensing terms*. Thus, while these policies technically require disclosure of something (patents) on an "ex ante" (before the fact) basis, they are not conventionally referred to as "ex ante" policies.

Moreover, much of the economics literature in this area discusses *ex ante* licensing disclosure approaches coupled with joint negotiation of license terms. *See* Damien Geradin, Anne Layne-Farrar, & A. Jorge Padilla, *The Ex Ante Auction Model for the Control of Market Power in Standard Setting Organizations* (working paper, Apr. 2007) (available at SSRN: http://ssrn.com/abstract=979393) and Anne Layne-Farrar, Gerard Llobet & A. Jorge Padilla, *Preventing Patent Hold up: An Economic Assessment of Ex Ante Licensing Negotiations in Standard Setting* (working paper, May 2008) (available at SSRN: http://ssrn.com/abstract=1129551). Such joint negotiation has been viewed by U.S. and European regulatory agencies as requiring a higher degree of scrutiny than mere *ex ante* licensing disclosure. *See* U.S. Dept. of Justice & U.S. Fed. Trade Comm., ANTITRUST ENFORCEMENT AND INTELLECTUAL PROPERTY RIGHTS: PROMOTING INNOVATION AND COMPETITION 53-56 (2007) (hereinafter "2007 DOJ/FTC Report") and European Commission, GUIDELINES ON THE APPLICABILITY OF ARTICLE 101 OF THE TREATY ON THE FUNCTIONING OF THE EUROPEAN UNION TO HORIZONTAL CO-OPERATION AGREEMENTS ¶299 (2011) (hereinafter "EC Horizontal Guidelines"). None of the SDOs examined in this study permit joint negotiation of licensing terms. For this reason, this report focuses on *ex ante* disclosure of licensing terms, and does not address *ex ante* negotiations.

[15] *See, e.g.,* Deborah Platt Majoras, *Recognizing the Procompetitive Potential of Royalty Discussions in Standard Setting*, Remarks prepared for "Standardization and the Law: Developing the Golden Mean for Global Trade", Stanford Law School, Sept. 23, 2005, at 8, U.S. Dept. of Justice, *Business Review Letter to VMEbus International Trade Association (VITA)* at 3 (Oct. 30, 2006) (hereinafter, "DOJ VITA Letter").

holders who would otherwise not be permitted to share royalty information with one another) and thus lead to collusion regarding royalty pricing.[16] On the implementer side, it is also claimed that requiring a patent holder to disclose its licensing terms *ex ante* might place too much power in the collective hands of licensees. That is, potential implementers of a standard, in negotiating license terms with a patent holder, could collectively exert anticompetitive pressure on the patent holder to reduce its royalties below their fair (or optimal) level.[17] Under this scenario, group pressure would tend to drive all royalty rates toward zero, resulting in the devaluation of patents covering the standard.[18] This type of improper buyer cartel or "oligopsony" is avoided when patent holders are permitted to negotiate license terms with implementers on a bilateral basis, constrained only by FRAND guidelines. These arguments do not assert that *ex ante* policies themselves violate antitrust laws, but that they are likely to encourage additional anticompetitive behavior within the SDO context. Regulatory agencies in both the U.S. and Europe have not, by and large, expressed concern with SDO *ex ante* policies absent further anticompetitive behavior by participants.[19] A detailed analysis of the antitrust and other legal critiques of *ex ante* policies is beyond the scope of this study.

      2.   *Process Criticisms.* Critics also contend that *ex ante* policies are both unnecessary and likely to be detrimental to the standards development process. *Ex ante* policies are unnecessary, they claim, because licenses to patents "essential" to the implementation of a standard are typically insufficient to meet implementers' commercial needs, and most implementers would prefer to negotiate broader, more inclusive license agreements with patent holders.[20] They also argue that *ex ante* disclosure of patents, already required by many SDOs, is sufficient to warn standards developers of potential patent "roadblocks" and enable them to work around patented technologies if they so desire; and the additional disclosure of licensing terms is unnecessary to achieve this purpose.[21] Finally, they contend that patent holders who participate in most SDOs are bound by commitments to license their essential patents on FRAND terms and willingly disclose their royalty rates and other licensing terms to potential implementers of a standard within the context of bilateral negotiations.[22]

      Critics go on to argue that the adoption of *ex ante* policies will have deleterious effects on the development of technical standards. One common contention in this vein is that the early disclosure of licensing terms will inappropriately focus standards developers' attention on patent licensing issues, making the overall standards development process more cumbersome, lengthy and expensive and distracting SDOs

---

[16] *See* 2007 DOJ/FTC Report, *supra* note 14, at 42-48.

[17] This type of anticompetitive buyer cartel is termed an "oligopsony". *See* 2007 DOJ/FTC Report, *supra* note 14, Skitol, *supra* note 6, at 735, Herman, *supra* note 11, at 38.

[18] Some commentators argue that royalty-free licensing is the most appropriate solution for interoperability standards. *See, e.g.*, Herman, *supra* note 11, at 37-38, Updegrove, *supra* note 10, at 11-12. An assessment of this argument, however, is beyond the scope of this paper.

[19] 2007 DOJ/FTC Report, *supra* note 14, at 53-55, EC Horizontal Guidelines, *supra* note 14, at ¶299.

[20] Herman, *supra* note 11, at 38 (arguing that implementers "generally do not want a license only to essential claims, but rather to all of the patent claims that their commercial implementations infringe...").

[21] *Id.* at 39.

[22] *Id.*

from the important work of standards development. Thus, while proponents of *ex ante* policies claim that such policies will *reduce* delays in the standardization process caused by the threat of patent hold-up, critics of *ex ante* policies argue that such policies will *lengthen* the standardization process and, consequently, reduce the number of valuable standards produced.[23] Critics also predict that the adoption of *ex ante* policies by SDOs will drive members away from these SDOs, either because members are unwilling to incur the additional costs imposed by such policies (i.e., increased legal support to evaluate and address licensing disclosures), because they feel that standards can be developed more efficiently elsewhere, or simply because they do not wish to comply with the early disclosure requirements of such policies.[24] In each of these cases, an SDO's loss of members would both weaken the SDO financially (due to loss of membership dues) and detract from the expertise that withdrawing participants could have contributed to the standardization process. On a related note, some have argued that *ex ante* policies may lead standards developers to settle for sub-optimal technologies in order to avoid the payment of royalties on patented, but superior, technologies.[25] In each of these cases, critics argue that an SDO's adoption of an *ex ante* policy is likely to weaken the technical output of the SDO and thus its value to members and to the economy as a whole.[26] Accordingly, it is the goal of this study to collect and analyze relevant empirical data that elucidates the correlation, if any, between the adoption of SDO *ex ante* policies and these predicted effects.

---

[23] *See* Richard S. Taffet, *Ex Ante Licensing in Standards Development – Myths and Reality* at 15 (presented to AIPLA Spring Meeting, May 4, 2006) (available at http://www.bingham.com/Media.aspx?MediaID=2742) ("[s]peed is of the essence in the development of technical standards ... [i]f it becomes necessary to evaluate the competitive effects of joint "ex ante" conduct, however, the ability to conclude the technical development of a standard could be tremendously inhibited"), Herman, *supra* note 11, at 39 ("collective consideration of patent licensing issues may unacceptably delay the standards development process"), 2007 DOJ/FTC Report, *supra* note 14, at 50, Skitol, *supra* note 6, at 734.

[24] *See* Michael A. Lindsay, *Negotiating Royalty or Other License Terms Before the Standard is Set* at 7 (presented at Am. Intell. Prop. L. Assn. 2009 Spring Meeting) (available at http://www.dorsey.com/files/upload/lindsay_negotiating_royalties_AIPLA_spring09.pdf), Herman, *supra* note 11, at 38; CLAUDIA TAPIA, INDUSTRIAL PROPERTY RIGHTS, TECHNICAL STANDARDS AND LICENSING PRACTICES (FRAND) IN THE TELECOMMUNICATIONS INDUSTRY 170 (2010), 2007 DOJ/FTC Report, *supra* note 14, at 50 (citing concerns of various panelists), Letter from Michele Herman, Davis Wright Tremaine LLP to Patrick Gallagher, National Institute of Standards and Technology, March 4, 2011 at 8 (available at http://standards.gov/standards_gov/sos_rfi_docs/26_Herman_DWTLLP.pdf) (hereinafter "DWT NIST RFP Response").

[25] *See* Taffet, *supra* note 23, at 15; TAPIA, *supra* note 24, at 178; DWT NIST RFP Response, *supra* note 24, at 8 (patent-holding innovators who leave an SDO due to the "hostile and costly" environment caused by its *ex ante* policy may "have the most to offer and contribute to the standards setting process", thus impacting the quality of standards developed in the SDO).

[26] *See* Michele Herman, *The Quandary of a Balanced IPR Policy*, LICENSING J., Oct. 2006, at 5, 7-8 (combining these three critiques: "[w]ithout the participation of such key contributors, who may possess key blocking IP applying to a standard, the resulting standard may take much longer to develop and be technically inferior").

G.   SDO Adoption and Consideration of Ex Ante Policies

Beginning around 2005, a number of SDOs in the U.S. and Europe began to consider the adoption of *ex ante* policies in one form or another.[27] Below is a brief summary of several of these efforts.

1.   *VITA.* The VMEBus International Trade Association (VITA), based in Scottsdale, Arizona, was incorporated in 1984 as a manufacturers' forum and support organization for the open VMEBus standard originally released by Motorola, Mostek, Signetics/Philips and Thomson CSF in 1981.[28] From 1981 to 1992, VITA continued to refine the VMEBus standard both independently and through participation in the IEEE P1014 Working Group. In 1992 VITA discontinued participation in the IEEE P1014 working group and formed the VITA Standards Organization (VSO), an independent organization within VITA, to evolve the VMEBus standard and develop additional standards of interest to its membership.[29] Shortly after its formation, VSO[30] was accredited by ANSI as an American National Standards developer and by the International Electrotechnical Commission (IEC) as a submitter of Industry Technical Agreements.[31] VITA standards today are used primarily in embedded computing systems designed for demanding environments including military, avionics, industrial and communications applications.

In the mid-1990s, VITA experienced two situations in which, late in the standards-development process, members disclosed patents deemed to be essential to the implementation of a VITA draft standard, and then demanded royalties that were "significantly higher than expected".[32] In each case, VITA engaged outside counsel to identify prior art potentially invalidating the disclosed patents and eventually succeeded in obtaining covenants from the patent holders not to assert such patents against implementers of VITA standards. In another instance, a VITA standard "was rendered commercially infeasible by the licensing terms demanded by the patent owner."[33]

In response to these incidents, after a series of internal deliberations, in 2006 VITA developed a draft *ex ante* policy. This policy requires that working group members holding patents "essential" to the implementation of a VITA standard disclose not only the existence of such patents, but also maximum applicable royalty rates and certain other

---

[27] *See* Updegrove, *supra* note 10, at 1-4 (describing events leading to the discussion of such policies).

[28] See VITA News Release, VITA and the VME Technology Community Celebrate 25th Anniversary, Oct. 23, 2006 (available at
http://www.vita.com/news/VITA%20and%20VME%20Technology%20Community%20Celebrate%2025th %20Anniversary%2010-2006.pdf).

[29] *See id.* and VSO Policies and Procedures, Rev. 2.6 – Nov. 30, 2009, at 3 (available at http://www.vita.com/vso-pp-r2d6.pdf).

[30] For purposes of clarity, throughout this report the term VITA will be used to refer both to VITA and VSO unless specific reference to VSO is required by the context.

[31] VITA Standards Organization (available at http://www.vita.com/vso-stds.html) (last visited May 29, 2011).

[32] DOJ VITA Letter, *supra* note 15, at 3 (citing Letter from Robert A. Skitol to Thomas O. Barnett, Assistant Atty. Gen., U.S. Dept. of Justice 2 (June 15, 2006) (hereinafter "Skitol Letter").

[33] *Id.* at 3-4 (citing Skitol Letter).

licensing restrictions.[34] A failure to disclose these terms will result in such patents being licensed to implementers of the standard on a royalty-free basis. Disclosures may be revised, but only if the revised disclosure are "less restrictive" than the ones they are intended to supersede. Patent holders are also be permitted, but not required, to accompany their disclosure with a sample license agreement. Recognizing the potential for antitrust liability arising from joint negotiation of licensing terms, the proposed policy expressly prohibits group licensing negotiations within the context of VITA.

In June 2006, VITA requested a business review of its proposed *ex ante* policy by the U.S. Department of Justice (DOJ). In October, the DOJ issued a business review letter in response to that request.[35] In its letter, the DOJ indicated that, unless a standards-setting policy is used to conceal naked price fixing or bid rigging, it is analyzed under the "rule of reason", in which both the policy's expected benefits and potential to restrain competition are examined and assessed.[36] In analyzing the proposed VITA *ex ante* policy, the DOJ concluded that the proposed *ex ante* disclosure of restrictive licensing terms would promote, rather than hinder, competition among patent holders.[37] It observed that such disclosures would enable working group members to evaluate technologies on both "technical merit and licensing terms," creating incentives for patent holders to compete in terms of royalties and other terms offered.[38] The agency concluded that the proposed VITA policy was:

> an attempt to preserve competition and thereby to avoid unreasonable patent licensing terms that might threaten the success of future standards and to avoid disputes over licensing terms that can delay adoption and implementation after standards are set.[39]

On January 17, 2007, the eligible VSO membership voted to adopt VITA's proposed *ex ante* policy by a majority of 35-2, with 12 abstentions.[40] Thereafter, in accordance with ANSI's Essential Requirements for developers of American National Standards, VITA submitted to the ANSI Executive Standards Council (ExSC) an application for re-accreditation.[41] VITA's re-accreditation application was opposed by Motorola, which argued, among other things, that VITA's *ex ante* policy failed to comply with ANSI's Essential Requirements and that such a policy would discourage

---

[34] Draft VITA Patent Policy (Oct. 30, 2006) (available at http://www.vita.com/disclosure/VITA%20Patent%20Policy%20section%2010%20draft.pdf).

[35] DOJ VITA Letter, *supra* note 15.

[36] *Id* at 8.

[37] *Id* at 10.

[38] *Id.* at 9.

[39] *Id.* at 10.

[40] Among the members opposing the approval of the *ex ante* policy was Motorola, which withdrew from VITA following this vote. Lindsay, *supra* note 24, at 7.

[41] Such re-accreditation is required each time an ANSI-accredited standards developer significantly alters its policies and procedures. Am. Natl. Standards Inst., ANSI Essential Requirements, Sec. 4.1.3 (2010) (available at http://publicaa.ansi.org/sites/apdl/Documents/Standards%20Activities/American%20National%20Standards/Procedures,%20Guides,%20and%20Forms/2010%20ANSI%20Essential%20Requirements%20and%20Related/2010%20ANSI%20Essential%20Requirements.pdf).

participation in VITA and thereby result in standards of lower quality. Notwithstanding this opposition, the ANSI ExSC approved VITA's re-accreditation request on May 28, 2007, requiring only minor adjustments to the *ex ante* policy.[42] Motorola thereafter appealed this decision, first to the ExSC and then to the ANSI Appeals Board, both of which declined to alter the ExSC decision to re-accredit VITA.[43] VITA's *ex ante* policy remains in effect today.

      2.   *IEEE*. The Institute for Electrical and Electronics Engineers (IEEE), based in Piscataway, New Jersey, traces its roots to 1884 and early professional engineering societies. Today, IEEE has over 350,000 individual members across the world and engages in a variety of activities including professional development, education, publishing and standards development. Standards development at IEEE is conducted through the IEEE Standards Association (IEEE-SA), an operating division that is accredited by ANSI as a developer of American National Standards. IEEE standards cover a broad of range of electrical and electronics applications including electrical safety, equipment disposal, batteries, power distribution and computer networking and communications.[44] Among the best-known IEEE standards today are the 802.3 Ethernet standard series and the 802.11 WiFi wireless networking standards.

      Prior to the mid-1990s, IEEE permitted the inclusion of patented technology in an IEEE standard if the patent holder agreed to FRAND licensing terms and assured "that the technology will be made available at nominal competitive costs to all who seek to use it for compliance with [the] standard."[45] Accordingly, patent holders were permitted to disclose licensing terms to IEEE on an *ex ante* basis. One prominent example of such a disclosure was made by National Semiconductor Corporation in 1994 with respect to certain patented technology that it proposed for inclusion in IEEE's 802.3 Fast Ethernet standard. National committed to IEEE that, if its NWay autodetection technology were incorporated into the standard, it would grant a license to any party implementing the standard for a flat fee of $1,000.[46] After considering the technical merits of various

---

[42] *See* VITA Press Release, VITA Secures ANSI Re-Accreditation, Modifies Patent Policy to Reflect Changes in Ex-Ante Disclosure (May 31, 2007) (available at http://www.vita.com/news/VITA%20Secures%20ANSI%20Re-Accreditation%205-2007.pdf).

[43] Final Notice, Appeal Filed by Motorola of the ANSI Executive Standards Council ("ExSC") Decision to Reaccredit the Procedures of VITA/VSO, an ANSI-Accredited Standards Developer (Jan. 22, 2008) (available at http://www.vita.com/disclosure/ANSI%20Appeals%20Board%20Decision%20in%20Motorola%20Appeal%2022Jan08.pdf).

[44] *See* IEEE Standards Association, Find Standards (available at http://standards.ieee.org/findstds/index.html) (last visited June 7, 2011).

[45] IEEE Standards Operations Manuals (1994) §6.3.1 (quoted in Lindsay, *supra* note 24, at 13).

[46] Decision and Order, *In the Matter of Negotiated Data Solutions LLC* (FTC, Sept. 9, 2008), FTC File No. 051-0094, Attachment A to Appendix C (Letter dated June 7, 1994 from Mark Grant, Director of Intellectual Property, National Semiconductor Corp. to Geoffrey Thompson, Chair, 802.3 Working Group, IEEE) (hereinafter "N-Data FTC Decision").

autodetection technologies, the IEEE working group chose NWay for inclusion in the Fast Ethernet standard, which was published in 1995.[47]

By 1996, however, the permissive disclosure clause of the IEEE policy had been removed,[48] and the policy approved in January 2005 expressly prohibited disclosing the terms or cost of licensing specific patents.[49] This trend, however, led to its own difficulties, and by the mid-2000s IEEE members were becoming dissatisfied with the vagueness of the organization's FRAND licensing commitment and their inability to compare cost factors when debating the merits of multiple proposed technologies for inclusion in a standard.[50] Thus, in early 2005, IEEE members proposed further revisions to IEEE's patent policy that, among other things, would require *ex ante* disclosure of maximum royalty rates and other licensing terms. After substantial discussion within IEEE,[51] in December 2006 final amendments to the policy were approved making this *ex ante* disclosure requirement optional rather than mandatory.[52]

Like VITA, IEEE requested a business review from the DOJ and, on April 30, 2007, the DOJ responded positively to IEEE's proposed *ex ante* policy. The DOJ recognized that IEEE working group members would be able to make "better informed decisions" by considering the cost of competing technologies along with their technical merits. It concluded that the IEEE proposal represented

> a sensible effort to preserve competition between technological alternatives before the standard is set in order to alleviate concern that commitments by patent holders to license on RAND terms are not sufficient to avoid disputes ..."[53]

The IEEE *ex ante* policy went into effect on April 30, 2007 and remains in effect today.

---

[47] *See* Lindsay, *supra* note 24, at 12-13. National's royalty commitment became the subject of dispute in 2008 after the relevant patents were assigned, in a series of transactions, to a third party that did not wish to honor National's original commitment. *See* N-Data FTC Decision, *supra* note 46.

[48] IEEE Standards Operations Manuals (1996).

[49] *See* IEEE-SA Standards Board Operations Manuals (2005) §5.3.9 (prohibiting, among other things, communications relating to "the validity, terms or cost of specific patent use"). *See also* Tor Winston, *Innovation and Ex Ante Consideration of Licensing Terms in Standard Setting*, U.S. Dept. Justice Economic Analysis Group Discussion Paper EAG 06-3 at 4 and n.7 (Mar. 2006) (available at http://www.justice.gov/atr/public/eag/221875.pdf).

[50] *See* U.S. Dept. of Justice, *Business Review Letter to Institute of Electrical and Electronics Engineers (IEEE)* at 4 (Apr. 30, 2007) (hereinafter, "DOJ IEEE Letter").

[51] *See* IEEE, PatCom Drafting Committee Documents (available at http://grouper.ieee.org/groups/pp-dialog/) (last accessed on June 8, 2011) (describing the multiple drafts, hundreds of written comments and marathon conference calls conducted during 2006 to reach agreement on amendments to the IEEE patent policy).

[52] A number of additional policy amendments were also introduced, including a requirement that a standardized form of Letter of Assurance (LOA) be used.

[53] DOJ IEEE Letter, *supra* note 50, at 11-12

3.   *ETSI*. The European Telecommunications Standards Institute (ETSI), based in Sophia-Antipolis, France, was formed in 1988 following a recommendation by the European Commission to supplement the two then-existing EU standards bodies, the European Committee for Standardization (CEN) and the European Committee for Electrotechnical Standardization (CENELEC).[54] ETSI focuses on standards for telecommunications, information technology and broadcasting and, unlike CEN, CENELEC and the more established International Telecommunications Union (ITU), ETSI's membership is open both to governmental actors and private industry. Today ETSI has more than 700 corporate members and is responsible for the widely-adopted GSM and UMTS mobile telephony standards.

ETSI proposed its first intellectual property policy in March 1993 in response to member concerns regarding patent hold-up.[55] This policy required ETSI members to grant FRAND licenses to all patents necessary to implement current and future ETSI standards, other than members who refused to agree to ETSI's licensing terms. This exclusion led to an investigation of ETSI's policy by the Commission in 1994 and a November 2004 revision of the draft policy that required disclosure of patents and broad FRAND licensing.[56] In 2005 the Commission again initiated an investigation of ETSI and its patent policy, this time fueled by concerns that the obligation of ETSI members to disclose essential patents was too weak.[57] ETSI amended its policy in November 2005 to address the Commission's concerns.[58] At the same time it formed a group to study additional policy revisions including the potential introduction of *ex ante* licensing disclosures, which the Commission had previously acknowledged as having the potential to offer "pro-competitive benefits."[59]

The ETSI group studying *ex ante* disclosure considered various options, and in 2006 proposed a model in which the *total* patent royalty payable with respect to a particular ETSI standard would be determined in advance, with resulting royalty payments being split among patent holders in a proportional manner.[60] The Commission, however, felt that such a system could preclude price competition and subvert the otherwise pro-competitive benefits of *ex ante* licensing disclosures.[61] Accordingly, ETSI

---

[54] *See* European Commission, Green Paper on the Development of the Common Market for Telecommunications Services and Equipment, COM (87) 290 final (June 13, 1987).

[55] *See* Maurits Dolmans, *Standards for Standards*, 26 FORDHAM INTL. L.J. 163, 181 (2002) and Rudi Bekkers & Joel West, *IPR Standardization Policies and Strategic Patenting in UMTS* at 5-6 (presented at 25th Celebration Conference 2008 on Entrepreneurship and Innovation – Organizations, Institutions, Systems and Regions).

[56] *See* Dolmans, *supra* note 55, at 179, n.65.

[57] *See* Pierre-André Dubois, *Standardization, FRAND Terms and Patent Misuse – Recent Developments*, EUROPEAN ANTITRUST REV. 2007 at 68.

[58] *See id.* at 68-69 (describing the change to Section 4.1 of the ETSI policy).

[59] *See* European Commission Press Release, Competition: Commission Welcomes Changes in ETSI IPR Rules to Prevent 'Patent Ambush', Dec. 12, 2005.

[60] *See* TAPIA, *supra* note 24, at 165.

[61] Letter dated June 21, 2006 from Ángel Tradacete Cocera, Director - Information, Communication and Media, European Commission Competition Directorate-General, to Karl Heinz Rosenbrock, ETSI Director General. Despite the Commission's lukewarm reaction to ETSI's collective royalty cap proposal, it

abandoned this approach and in 2007 adopted a voluntary *ex ante* policy.[62] To date, however, it appears that no *ex ante* licensing disclosures have been made under ETSI's policy.[63]

4.   *Consortia (W3C and NGMN).* While the *ex ante* policies at VITA and IEEE have to date received the most attention from U.S. commentators and regulators, a number of other organizations have adopted or considered policies designed to alleviate the risk of patent hold-up in standards-development through early notice of licensing terms. Several organizations, most notably the Worldwide Web Consortium (W3C)[64] have adopted policies requiring that participants holding patents essential to the implementation of a standard license these patents to all implementers of the standard on a royalty-free basis. Such royalty-free (RF)[65] policies, mandating royalty rates of zero (except under certain exceptional circumstances), could be considered a sub-species of *ex ante* policies, as the royalty rate is known to implementers as soon as essential patents are disclosed.   Other groups, such as open software standards-developer OASIS, permit technical committees to determine, upon formation, whether they will require FRAND or RF licensing commitments from their participants.[66]

Consortia have also experimented with formal *ex ante* policies. One such group, the Next-Generation Mobile Networks consortium (NGMN), was formed in 2006 by mobile telephone network operators not to develop standards, but to advance operator interests and technical requirements within telecommunications-focused SDOs such as ETSI.[67]   Although NGMN itself does not develop standards, it requires each of its members to disclose to a trusted third party the royalties and other material terms on which it would be willing to license its patents essential to the implementation of certain industry standards.[68]   The trusted party then aggregates and anonymizes this royalty information and provides it in a confidential report to the NGMN membership.[69]

---

remains supportive of *ex ante* disclosure structures generally. *See* EC Horizontal Guidelines, *supra* note 14, at ¶299.

[62]   ETSI,   Ex   Ante   Disclosures   of   Licensing   Terms   (available   at http://www.etsi.org/WebSite/AboutETSI/IPRsInETSI/Ex-ante.aspx) (last visited June 7, 2011).

[63]   *See* ETSI, List of Ex Ante Disclosures of Licensing Terms (available at http://www.etsi.org/WebSite/AboutETSI/IPRsInETSI/Ex-ante-list-of-disclosures.aspx) (last visited June 7, 2011) (no disclosures listed).

[64]   www.w3c.org.

[65]   A number of variants of RF policies exist, including so-called RAND-RF or RAND-Z policies, which require the imposition of otherwise RAND terms, but with no royalty or other consideration charged. *See* ABA Manual, *supra* note 8, at 56-58.

[66]   OASIS Intellectual Property Rights (IPR) Policy (available at http://www.oasis-open.org/policies-guidelines/ipr#licensing_req) (last visited June 6, 2011).

[67]   *See* Next Generation Mobile Networks, Mission and Vision (available at http://www.ngmn.org/aboutus.html) (last visited June 6, 2011).

[68]   NGMN, Participant Application Form, Annex 2 – IPR Guidelines, §2.a (available at http://www.ngmn.org/fileadmin/user_upload/Downloads/Membership/NGMN_IPR_Guidelines.pdf).   The selected standards include 3GPP Long Term Evolution (LTE), IEEE 802.16M, IEEE 802.20 and 3GPP2 Ultra Mobile Broadband. Id. at §1.i.

[69]   *Id.* at §7.

The intent of this procedure was to encourage full and frank disclosure of royalty rates by ensuring that no individual member's licensing terms became known to the others (its competitors). Each member, however, would learn the aggregate royalties that would be payable with respect to each standard of interest and thus, presumably, have a basis on which to compare the economic desirability of these different standards. It is unclear whether these goals have been achieved in practice. First, it has been reported that the aggregate royalty rates for different standards have been surprisingly high (by one account, 130% of the net sales price of the equipment in question).[70] Others have noted that the reported royalty structures have been unduly complex and difficult to compare, and that the trusted party's reports have extended to hundreds of pages, making them cumbersome and difficult to use.

Thus, while NGMN has taken positive steps toward the implementation of an *ex ante* policy, the aggregated and anonymized nature of the reported information and the fact that NGMN itself does not develop standards, make it an unlikely candidate for assessing the effect of an *ex ante* policy on the standards-development processes addressed by this study.

5.   *IETF and "Informal"* Ex Ante *Approaches.* The Internet Engineering Task Force (IETF)[71] is the primary developer of Internet architecture, transport and security protocols, specifications and standards worldwide. The IETF grew out of early U.S. government/academic projects that designed the basic architecture of the packet-switched network that eventually became the Internet. Since 1992, IETF's activities have been conducted under the auspices of the non-profit Internet Society, based in Reston, Virginia and Geneva, Switzerland. Like IEEE, participation in IETF is on an individual basis, though many companies sponsor the attendance and participation of their employees in IETF activities. In recent years, at any given time over a hundred different working groups have been operational within IETF. IETF was responsible for the development of fundamental Internet protocols including TCP, IP, HTTP and MIME, and has never sought accreditation from ANSI as a developer of American National Standards.

The IETF's policy regarding patents was initially developed in 1992 as part of RFC 1310,[72] and contained a FRAND or RF licensing requirement based on the then-current ANSI Essential Requirements. The basis for the current IETF patent policy, however, was established in 1996 as part of RFC 2026, and only requires that participants disclose the existence of known intellectual property rights covering contributions to IETF, but does not require that the patent holder grant any license at all to implementers

---

[70] TAPIA, *supra* note 24, at 194.

[71] www.ietf.org.

[72] For historical reasons, IETF standards are designated as "Requests for Comments" or "RFCs". In the IETF, both technical standards and documents setting forth the organization's rules and policies are published as RFCs.

of the standard.[73] While more detailed, IETF's current policy contained in RFC 3979 and subsequent addenda preserves this disclosure-only approach.[74]

While requiring that patent disclosures contain certain specified information (such as patent and patent application numbers, dates, affected standards, and the like), IETF does not require that such disclosures be made in any particular format. Thus, IETF participants are free to include additional information in their patent disclosures, so long as this information does not contravene any express IETF requirement (e.g., alterations to copyright permissions). Given this freedom, many IETF participants have elected to include information regarding their licensing intentions in patent disclosures. This licensing information can include commitments to license on FRAND or royalty-free terms, discussions of specific clauses that will be applicable to licenses, and broad commitments not to assert patents in enumerated contexts. And while IETF does not require a licensing commitment or *ex ante* disclosure of licensing terms, it does not *prohibit* the disclosure of this information. I refer to this combination of tacit approval by the organization and established practice within the community as an "informal" *ex ante* approach.

III.   Study Aims and Methodology

A.   *Study Aims*

The aim of this study is to collect and analyze empirical data relevant to the effect of *ex ante* policies on standards development. We have organized our data collection and analysis in accordance with predictions made by critics of *ex ante* policies regarding the potential effects of such policies on standardization processes and efficacy. In particular, our data collection and analysis has been organized around the following six assertions relating to *ex ante* policies:

1.   *Ex ante* policies will reduce standardization activity.

2.   *Ex ante* policies will cause standards to take longer to develop.

3.   *Ex ante* policies will require standards developers to devote more time to standardization activities.

4.   *Ex ante* policies will cause members to withdraw from SDOs that adopt them.

5.   *Ex ante* policies will cause standards to decrease in quality.

---

[73] Internet Engineering Task Force, *RFC 2026 – The Internet Standards Process – Revision 3* (Oct. 1996), §10.3.1.6.
[74] Internet Engineering Task Force, *RFC 3979 –Intellectual Property Rights in IETF Technology* (Mar. 2005).

6.   *Ex ante* policies will depress patent royalty rates.

B.   *Methodology*

1.   *SDOs Selected.* As VITA is the only SDO to adopt a mandatory *ex ante* requirement that has been considered by the U.S. Department of Justice, VITA was the primary focus of our data collection and analysis. Much VITA data is not publicly-available, thus we relied heavily on the cooperation of VITA's executive director and staff in providing us with requested information.

Like VITA, IEEE adopted an *ex ante* policy in early 2007 and obtained a business review letter from the Department of Justice. Unlike VITA, however, IEEE's *ex ante* policy permits *ex ante* disclosure of licensing terms, but does not require it. In this respect, IEEE presents an interesting contrast to VITA. Accordingly, we collected data relating to IEEE. Much IEEE data is publicly-available on the organization's web site (www.ieee.org). To the extent that data was not publicly-available, we were able to obtain limited information from IEEE staff. However, as noted below, some IEEE data was either unavailable or not made accessible to us.

In addition to VITA and IEEE we collected data from IETF, which has not adopted an express *ex ante* policy but which, as noted above, permits informal *ex ante* disclosures. Given the size and prominence of IETF, we believe that it can be viewed as representative of general trends within the ICT standards-development community. Most IETF data is publicly-available on the Internet (www.ietf.org), making it a common subject of academic analysis and commentary. We did not seek non-public data from IETF.

We did not collect or analyze data relating to ETSI, NGMN or other SDOs, for a number of reasons. First, we felt that our primary emphasis, at this stage, should be on organizations with a primary connection to the U.S. Second, the *ex ante* policies of VITA and IEEE have received the greatest attention from U.S. commentators, most likely due to the issuance of DOJ business review letters to each of these organizations. ETSI and NGMN have received less attention from U.S. commentators and regulators, and have played a smaller role in the *ex ante* debate as it has evolved in the U.S. Third, the *ex ante* policies and practices of ETSI and NGMN are not condusive to empirical study for a number of reasons. ETSI, as noted above, has to-date received no disclosures under its *ex ante* policy. NGMN is not an SDO and does not develop standards. Thus, the predicted effects of *ex ante* policies on NGMN would be difficult to compare with the effects on SDOs such as VITA and IEEE. Moreover, the aggregated nature of NGMN's *ex ante* disclosures make them still more difficult to compare to the others. As noted above, we included IETF in this study for comparative purposes, as a large, well-respected SDO in the same industry category as VITA and IEEE, with all relevant data available in the public domain and with the benefit of numerous academic studies to use as bases for comparison. For these reasons, we elected to focus this study on VITA, IEEE and IETF.

2.   *Time Period.* As our goal was to examine the effect that the adoption of *ex ante* policies had on SDO procedures and practices, we generally collected and analyzed data from 2004 to 2010, three years before and after the adoption of the VITA and IEEE policies in 2007. In categories in which VITA lacked relevant data for 2004 (e.g., standards adopted), we extended our start date to 2003. With respect to patent and licensing disclosures, we limited our review to the period 2007-2010, as both VITA and IEEE adopted their *ex ante* policies in early 2007, and data prior to that period was not useful for comparison.

3.   *Historical Data.*

a.   *Disclosures.* For each of VITA, IEEE and IETF we reviewed formal disclosures of patent information made from 2007 to 2010. Formal disclosures are those submitted directly to the SDO through its established patent disclosure mechanisms, and do not include unofficial notices, letters, e-mail discussions, litigation filings or other means of communication.

VITA does not publish disclosures made under its *ex ante* policy. However, following submission of VITA standards to ANSI for approval as American National Standards, ANSI has published some VITA disclosures on its web site.[75] In order to analyze information regarding both ANSI-approved and draft VITA standards, we obtained copies of all *ex ante* disclosures directly from VITA.[76] Due to the non-public nature of VITA disclosures pertaining to draft standards, we agreed not to disclose the specific terms of VITA *ex ante* disclosures to the extent they are not already publicly-available via the ANSI web site.

With respect to IEEE, we obtained this information from the Letters of Assurance available at the "IEEE-SA Records of IEEE Standards-Related Patents" found on the IEEE public website.[77] With respect to IETF, we obtained disclosure information from the list of IPR Disclosures found on the IETF public website.[78]

In each SDO, disclosures are permitted with respect to both draft and approved standards. We counted all such disclosures equally, and our statistics relating to "Standards Covered by Patent/Licensing Disclosures" reflect disclosures covering both standards starts and approved standards. While all standards starts may not ultimately lead to approved standards, whether or not a standards activity will lead to an approved standard is not known at the time of disclosure, making the eventual approval of the standard somewhat irrelevant to the decision whether or not to disclose. In many cases, individual disclosures state that they apply to multiple standards and/or draft standards.

---

[75]   SDO   patent   disclosures   submitted   to   ANSI   can   be   found   at http://publicaa.ansi.org/sites/apdl/Patent%20Letters/Forms/AllItems.aspx.

[76] Materials provided on March 1, 2011. Some of this information is publicly-accessible on the web site of the American National Standards Institute (ANSI) at www.ansi.org.

[77]   http://standards.ieee.org/db/patents/index.html.   As of April 2011, this link was moved to http://standards.ieee.org/about/sasb/patcom/patents.html.

[78] https://datatracker.ietf.org/ipr/. This information can also be accessed by searching for the RFC number in the IETF's online IPR Disclosure database at https://datatracker.ietf.org/ipr/search/.

We counted separately each individual standard or draft standard to which a particular disclosure purported to apply. In the case of IETF, if disclosures identified different versions of an Internet-Draft, we counted each different Internet-Draft version.

In most cases, each disclosure cites a single patent. In a minority of cases, however, disclosures cite multiple patents, including non-U.S. counterparts, divisional and continuation applications. Thus, although, as noted above, we counted the number of separate standards cited by each disclosure, we did not separately count each patent cited in each disclosure. We adopted this approach because the focus of our study is on numbers of standards rather than numbers of patents. Thus, so long as a disclosure identifies all *standards* implicated by the disclosed patent(s), it is not meaningful whether the patent holder claims to have one or a dozen patents that are essential to the implementation of that standard. We excluded from the IEEE count of disclosures Letters of Assurance that simply stated that the submitter was not aware of any patents an option permitted by the IEEE form Letter of Assurance), as these are not patent disclosures of the type under review.

In describing the terms of *ex ante* licensing disclosures, our use of the term "Royalty-Free" includes disclosures stating that patents will be licensed on a royalty-free basis, that the patent holder will not assert patents against implementers of the standard or that no license is required to operate under such patents. The addition of reciprocity, defensive suspension and other customary terms of standards-based FRAND licenses to such Royalty-Free declarations, and the offer of optional royalty-bearing terms in addition to royalty-free terms, did not change our classification of a disclosure as Royalty-Free. We did not account for the fact that at IETF all computer code included within standards is licensed under the open source BSD license. When counting disclosures that included non-royalty license terms, we did not count disclosures that simply listed FRAND commitments (as most IEEE Letters of Assurance do). We counted a disclosure as including non-royalty licensing terms if it included an attached license agreement or described non-royalty terms other than simple FRAND assurances, such as reciprocity, defensive suspension, field limitations, or the like.

b.   *Standards Started.* For each of VITA, IEEE and IETF we determined the number of new standards-development activities initiated during each year from 2004 to 2010. IEEE and IETF data were obtained from the public web sites of each organization.[79] VITA data were obtained directly from the organization.[80]

For VITA standards, we counted all standards started during each year studied. When two related standards were started on the same date (e.g., VITA 49.0 and 49.1, both of which were started on June 24, 2004), we considered these to be separate

---

[79] IEEE Standards Status Report obtained from http://standards.ieee.org/db/status/status.txt on Oct. 14, 2010 (now available at http://standards.ieee.org/develop/project/status.html). IETF data was manually compiled from the IETF Datatracker at https://datatracker.ietf.org for standards approved through Nov. 30, 2010.

[80] Data provided by VITA on Apr. 18, 2011.

standards, as each potentially has a separate technical implementation, product base and, in theory, patent coverage.[81]

For IEEE standards, we deemed the "start" date to be the date on which the Project Authorization Request for the standard was approved. We did not count as separate standards 26 different corrigenda, as these are generally technical corrections to existing standards. Five other "standards" were also excluded where the description noted that only minor changes were being made to existing standards.

For IETF, we considered the publication of a new IETF Internet-Draft to constitute the "start" of a new standardization process. An Internet-Draft is a draft document that may progress through the IETF standardization process. Many Internet-Drafts, however, do not advance to become IETF standards (designated as Requests for Comments or RFCs), and many are informational in nature and are never intended to advance along the "standards track". In addition, many Internet-Drafts that are intended to be standards-track documents are eventually combined with other Internet-Drafts or superseded, by different technical approaches reflected in different Internet-Drafts. Thus, there are many more Internet-Drafts published in any given year than standards adopted at IETF. Nevertheless, for IETF, the publication of new Internet-Drafts seemed best to reflect the number of new standardization activities begun during any given time period. As this data is being used primarily to compare trends among VITA, IEEE and IETF, the absolute number of new standards starts at IETF is not itself as significant as the *changes* in the number of new standards starts year to year.

In order to measure the number of new Internet Drafts published each year at IETF, we reviewed the "IETF Chair Report" of each IETF meeting starting from IETF 59 (Seoul, February 29-March 4, 2004) and ending with IETF 79 (Beijing, November 7-12, 2010).[82] Beginning with IETF 61, each such IETF Chair Report includes a slide that notes how many new Internet-Drafts were started since the last meeting. Because IETF meetings are held in (roughly) March, July/August and November of each year, and the number of new Internet-Drafts reported are since the last meeting, the "annual" totals that we calculated for IETF reflect figures from November to November of each year, rather than a true calendar year. In addition, because the IETF Chair Reports did not begin to report new Internet-Drafts until IETF 61 (November 2004), we had incomplete data for 2004. In order to estimate the total number of new Internet-Drafts for 2004, we extrapolated full-year data from the partial-year data presented in November 2004.

      c.   *Standards Approved*. For each of VITA, IEEE and IETF we determined the number of standards approved during each year from 2003 to 2010. IEEE and IETF data were obtained from the public web sites of each organization. VITA data were obtained directly from the organization.[83]

---

[81] In contrast, when computing average time to standardization, we combined related standards so as not to double-count a single standardization process.

[82] A list of these meeting links can be found at http://www.ietf.org/meeting/proceedings.html.

[83] Data provided by VITA on Mar. 1, 2011.

For VITA standards, we counted all standards adopted during each year studied. When two related standards were approved on the same date (e.g., VITA 49.0 and 49.1, both of which were approved on May 26, 2009), we considered these to be separate standards.[84]

For IEEE standards, we deemed the date of "approval" to be the date on which the IEEE-SA Board approved the standard. We did not count as separate standards 26 different corrigenda, as these are generally technical corrections to existing standards. Five other "standards" were also excluded where the description noted that only extremely minor changes were being made to existing standards. In many of these cases, the standard was both proposed and approved on the same day or very shortly thereafter.

For IETF standards, we identified each Request for Comments (RFC), the official designation for IETF standards, published during 2004 to 2010. The IETF Datatracker web site[85] displays the "History" of each such RFC. From the History tab for each RFC, we identified the date on which such RFC was "Approved – announcement sent" or "Approved – announcement to be sent". We did not use the RFC publication date, as this date was often significantly later than the approval date due to delays associated with the RFC Editor function and not related to the IETF standardization process.[86]

        d.   *Standardization Time.* For each of VITA, IEEE and IETF we determined the average time between the introduction of a draft standard and its final approval by the SDO for all standards approved from 2003 to 2010. IEEE and IETF data were obtained from the public web sites of each organization. VITA data were obtained directly from the organization. For purposes of this analysis, we did not consider draft standards documents that did not result in approved standards as of December 31, 2010.

For each VITA standard adopted between 2003 and 2010, we measured the number of days between the introduction of the original technical proposal and the resulting standard's final approval, then calculated the average number of days required for adoption of all standards during each such year. For purposes of this calculation, we combined related standards that were started and approved on substantially the same dates. For example, VITA 48.0, 48.1 and 48.2 were each started on January 21, 2004. VITA 48.0 and 48.2 were approved on June 22, 2010 and VITA 48.1 was approved on July 7, 2010, approximately two weeks later. Given that these three standards relate to a common set of specifications and were developed as part of a single standardization process, all three are considered as a single standard for purposes of determining the length of VITA standardization processes, notwithstanding that the approval of VITA 48.1 required two additional weeks at the end of a six-year standardization process.

---

[84] In contrast, when computing average time to standardization, we combined related standards so as not to double-count a single standardization process.

[85] http://datatracker.ietf.org.

[86] This distinction is discussed by Simcoe in his study of IETF standards. Tim Simcoe, *Delay and de jure Standardization: Exploring the Slowdown in Internet Standards Development* in STANDARDS AND PUBLIC POLICY 260 (2006) (available at http://www.rotman.utoronto.ca/strategy/research/working%20papers/Simcoe%20-%20Delays.pdf).

For IEEE standards, we measured the number of days between the approval of a standard's Project Authorization Request and IEEE-SA board approval. In cases in which a standard was proposed and dropped without board approval, then subsequently resubmitted and approved, we considered this to be a single approval process measured from the initial Project Authorization Request. If the standard was approved by the board and later amended in a separate approval process, we counted it as two different standards with two different approval periods.

For IETF Standards, we measured the number of days between the publication of the initial Internet-Draft referencing the standard and the approval of the resulting RFC for publication. When subsequent Internet-Drafts replaced or superseded earlier Internet-Drafts relating to the same standards activity, we counted from the initial Internet-Draft publication.

e. *Membership Data.* For each of VITA and IETF we compiled overall membership data, specifically the number of members joining and withdrawing from each organization, for each annual period from 2004 to 2010. We were unable to obtain comparable membership data from IEEE.[87]

With respect to VITA, we obtained a current list of VITA members from the organization.[88] For prior years, we referred to the roster of VITA members on publicly-archived versions of VITA's public website for each year from 2004 to 2009.[89] We recorded the number of members who joined and withdrew from the organization in each year and calculated the net change in membership for each such year. For the reasons discussed below, we made a number of adjustments to the raw data that we used to calculate net year-to-year membership changes.

First, VITA permits related entities (e.g., parent, subsidiary and sibling companies) to maintain separate memberships in the organization, so long as each such entity pays the required membership dues. For purposes of this study, we treated related entities as a single member. We adopted this approach because the purpose of this analysis is to measure the effect of the adoption of VITA's *ex ante* policy on membership in the organization. Because, in our view, intellectual property decisions are likely to be made centrally rather than at the subsidiary level, treating related entities as separate

---

[87] Unlike VITA and IETF, IEEE is a broadly-focused trade association that conducts numerous activities in addition to technical standards-setting. Overall membership in IEEE is in the range of 350,000 individuals and entities (see http://www.ieee.org/about/corporate/annual_report.html). Standards-setting within IEEE is conducted within the IEEE Standards Association (IEEE-SA), which does not publish separate membership lists or statistics.

[88] List provided Dec. 23, 2010.

[89] We accessed archived versions of the VITA website using the Internet Archive http://www.archive.org/web/web.php. The specific URLs accessed were http://web.archive.org/web/*/http://www.vita.com and http://waybackmachine.org/*/http://www.vita.com. We collected VITA membership data from the VITA membership pages archived for the following dates: Dec. 5, 2000, June 28, 2001, Nov. 29, 2002, Dec. 20, 2003, Dec. 29, 2004, Dec. 23, 2005, Dec. 27, 2006, Oct. 12, 2007, Dec. 17, 2008, and Mar. 16, 2009.

members could give undue weight to the decisions made by these entities.[90] A total of eleven different groups of related entities (two entities in ten cases and three entities in one case) were thus counted as eleven individual members. By the same token, when one entity withdrew and was replaced by a related entity during the same year, we counted neither the departure of the first entity nor the addition of the second entity as a change in membership.

Second, based on information provided by VITA staff,[91] we disregarded (for counting purposes) the departure of VITA members due to their acquisition by other VITA members (as such departures would not be indicative of a desire by the departing members not to remain in the organization). In each year measured, between two and ten departures were disregarded for this reason.[92] If, however, a VITA member departed the organization following its acquisition by a non-member, this departure was counted and no adjustment was made to the departure count. Given the various adjustments to the VITA membership count described above, we felt that presenting either raw or adjusted membership figures would be less informative than presenting the net *changes* in VITA membership year over year, using 2004 as a baseline.

With respect to IETF, we compiled meeting attendee information from North American IETF meetings held between 2004 and 2010, as listed on the IETF public web site.[93] North American meetings were selected in order to provide the most consistent basis for comparison with VITA, the membership of which is drawn primarily from North America.

---

[90] For example, VITA membership records for 2005 and other years list both Lockheed Martin and Lockheed Martin Integrated Systems as members. Based on our experience, decisions regarding intellectual property policy within large organizations are typically made by a centralized general counsel's office and are followed by all divisions and subsidiaries within the corporate group.

[91] Telephone Interview of Ray Alderman, Mar. 17, 2011 (conducted by Contreras).

[92] The table below shows the number of VITA departures per year that were disregarded because the VITA member was acquired by an entity that was already a VITA member:

Year	Disregarded Departures (M&A)
2005	7
2006	10
2007	2
2008	8
2009	2
2010	5

Alderman Interview, *supra* note 91.

[93] http://www.ietf.org/meeting/past.html. The meetings selected were: 60th IETF (Aug. 2004, San Diego, CA); 62nd IETF (Mar. 2005, Minneapolis, MN); 65th IETF (Mar. 2006, Dallas, TX); 69th IETF (Jul. 2007, Chicago, IL); 71st IETF (Mar. 2008, Philadelphia, PA); 74th IETF (Mar. 2009, San Francisco, CA); and 77th IETF (Mar. 2010, Anaheim, CA).

Unlike VITA, IETF membership is on an individual, rather than a corporate basis. Thus multiple individuals employed by the same company can, and do, attend IETF meetings, and each is counted as a separate attendee. We made no adjustments to IETF attendance data to account for multiple attendees from the same company or otherwise, as determining such information was not feasible. While IETF meeting attendance does not provide a perfect basis for comparison with VITA corporate membership, IETF attendance rates are believed to be indicative of overall trends in SDO participation in the ICT sector during the period under review.

f. *Citation Data.* For each VITA standard approved between 2003 and 2010,[94] we conducted a Google web search and recorded the number of "hits" returned by Google. The search was conducted on May 25, 2011. Each search query was constructed in a uniform manner using the term "VITA", the numerical designation of the standard and all words from the title of the standard excluding articles, conjunction, punctuation marks and the words "draft", "standard" and "specification". If words were repeated within the title of the standard we did not repeat them in the query. For example, the search query constructed for VITA 58.0 "Line Replaceable Integrated Electronics Chassis Draft Standard" was "VITA 58.0 Line Replaceable Integrated Electronics Chassis". We plotted the results on a natural logarithmic scale (y-axis) against date of adoption (x-axis).

4. *Survey Data.* In order to provide greater context to the historical data described above, we conducted an online survey of all current VITA VSO participants (88 individuals).[95]

a. *Administration; Response Rate.* The survey included 26 questions, most of which called for closed-ended, multiple choice responses (described in more detail below).[96] The survey was conducted between March 3 and March 18, 2011 using the Survey Monkey online survey administration tool.[97] An initial e-mail solicitation containing a link to the secure survey web site and privacy statement was sent to each VSO member by the VITA Executive Director. Two short reminder notices were also sent during the course of the survey. No incentives were offered to respondents other than an offer to share the results of the study. A total of 47 responses were received (response rate 53.4%; margin of error 9.8%[98]).

b. *Demographic Data.* The survey included 14 demographic questions. Respondents were asked to report the industry sector of their employer (product vendor, product purchaser, regulator, academic, other), their job function

---

[94] We excluded one standard, VITA 57.1r1, from this calculation, as this standard is labeled solely as a revision to the existing standard VITA 57.1 and the 1r1 version, standing alone, received no hits.

[95] Though we sought permission to survey participants in the IEEE Standards Association, IEEE declined this request. In a future study, it may be desirable to survey a broader cross-section of ICT standardization professionals.

[96] Approved by Washington University in St. Louis, Human Research Protection Office (HRPO), Feb. 11, 2011 (IRB ID# 201102234).

[97] www.surveymonkey.com.

[98] Calculated using standard margin of error formula for finite populations: N=88, n=47.

(engineering, business/management, legal, marketing, other), and their general level of experience with technical standardization, patents and patent litigation. Several questions also asked for information regarding the respondent's practices in connection with standards-development at VITA, including the frequency with which the respondent checks patent and licensing disclosures made in connection with VITA standards under development. A summary of the demographic characteristics of the survey respondents is contained in the Data Appendix.

      c.   *VITA-Specific Questions.* The survey included 12 questions that solicited information regarding the respondent's experiences with, and impressions of, standards-development at VITA both before and after adoption of the 2007 *ex ante* policy. Questions required the respondent both to compare standards-development at VITA with standards-development at other SDOs, and to compare standards-development at VITA before adoption of the *ex ante* policy with standards-development at VITA following adoption of the *ex ante* policy. Variables measured included speed of standards-development at VITA, length of time spent by the respondent on VITA standards-development and quality of VITA standards. Additional questions asked for information regarding the respondent's actions taken in response to *ex ante* licensing disclosures, and to the adoption of the VITA *ex ante* policy.

      d.   *Analysis.*[99] Descriptive and bivariate analyses were conducted on all closed-ended survey questions using SAS version 9.2 for Windows. Bivariate associations between respondent experience levels and other demographic data and perceptions regarding the effect of the *ex ante* policy on VITA's standardization processes were analyzed. Significance was assessed at $p < 0.05$. Due to the small sample size (n=47), Fisher's exact test was used to assess bivariate associations.

---

[99] Analysis conducted by Dr. Melody Goodman, School of Medicine, Washington University in St. Louis.

IV.   Findings and Analysis

A.   *SDO Patent and Licensing Disclosures.*

1.   *Comparative Disclosure Data.* As discussed in Section II.G above, VITA, IEEE and IETF each address *ex ante* disclosures of licensing information in different ways: VITA requires *ex ante* licensing disclosures, IEEE expressly permits them, and IETF permits free-form disclosures that may, and sometimes do, include licensing information. Table A.1 below compares each organization's patent and licensing disclosures from 2007 (the year in which VITA and IEEE approved their *ex ante* policies) through 2010.

Table A.1
Comparison of SDO Disclosure Patterns (2007-2010)

	VITA	IEEE	IETF
Standards Approved	18	333	1,243
Total Patent Disclosures	7	349	481
Standards Covered by Disclosures	7	103	594
Ratio of Standards Covered by Patent Disclosures : Approved Standards	1 : 2.6	1 : 3.2	1 : 2.1
Non-Royalty Licensing Term Disclosures	7	33	276
Royalty-Free/Non-Assert (RF) Disclosures	1	11	283
Non-Zero Royalty Disclosures	6	2	0
Total *Ex Ante* Licensing Disclosures	7	39	366
Ex Ante Licensing Disclosures as % of All Patent Disclosures	100%	11%	76%
Standards Covered by *Ex Ante* Licensing Disclosures	7	35	389
Ratio of Standards Covered by *Ex Ante* Licensing Disclosures : Approved Standards	1 : 2.6	1 : 9.5	1 : 3.2

A number of observations emerge from this data. First, the percentage of each organization's standards (both approved and draft) that are covered by *patent* disclosures is surprisingly consistent across the three organizations, despite the wide variance in their activity levels. Thus at IETF, which approved 1,243 standards during the period, patents were disclosed with respect to 594 separate standards activities, at a ratio of 1:2.1, while at VITA, 7 patent disclosures were made with a total of 18 approved standards, at a ratio of 1:2.6, and at IEEE, the comparable ratio of 1:3.2 was only slightly higher. This level of consistency suggests both that the number of patents applicable to standardization activities across the ICT sector is relatively constant, and that participants in ICT standardization activities comply with SDO patent disclosure requirements at a relatively consistent rate.

The divergence among the three SDOs becomes apparent in the lower portion of Table A.1, which compares *ex ante* licensing disclosures.[100] At VITA, where *ex ante* licensing disclosures are required, each patent disclosure (n=7) also contained licensing information. At IETF, 366 of 481 patent disclosures (76%) contained licensing information, whereas at IEEE, only 11%, or 39 of 349 disclosures contained licensing information. We identified two distinct types of *ex ante* licensing information: royalty-related terms and non-royalty terms beyond simple FRAND assurances. In some cases, *ex ante* disclosures contained both royalty-related and non-royalty information.

Royalty-related terms included both royalty-free licensing commitments and non-zero royalty rates. The disclosure of non-zero royalty rates was observed almost exclusively at VITA, where 86% (n=6) of all *ex ante* disclosures contained a non-zero maximum royalty. At IETF there were no non-zero royalty disclosures, and at IEEE, where such disclosures are permitted but not required, there were only two (6% of all *ex ante* disclosures).[101] These observations suggest that, even at SDOs in which *ex ante* disclosure is permitted, participants that wish to license their patents on a royalty-bearing basis may be reluctant to disclose royalty information unless compelled to do so by an express *ex ante* policy.[102] The same is not the case, however, with respect to royalty-free licensing commitments, which participants seem willing to disclose voluntarily, even absent a policy-based requirement to do so. Thus, while IETF had no royalty-bearing disclosures at all, 59% (n=283) of all IETF patent disclosures contained royalty-free licensing commitments.[103]

Data regarding the *ex ante* disclosure of non-royalty licensing terms is also worth consideration. At IEEE, most of the *ex ante* licensing disclosures (67%, n=26) were of non-royalty information only (e.g., reciprocity, defensive suspension, etc.),[104] and a full 57% (n=276) of all IETF patent disclosures included licensing information beyond a simple FRAND or royalty-free licensing statement. Thus, while the principal debate concerning *ex ante* disclosure policies has focused on the disclosure of royalty rates, it appears that SDO participants also have an interest in disclosing, and reviewing disclosures of, non-royalty licensing terms.[105]

---

[100] As discussed in Section III.B.3.a, *supra*, we consider *ex ante* licensing disclosures to constitute any disclosure of licensing terms beyond a simple FRAND commitment, and may include royalty-related terms and/or other licensing terms.

[101] One of the two *ex ante* non-zero royalty disclosures made to IEEE was submitted by Negotiated Data Solutions (N-Data) following a decision by the Federal Trade Commission. *See* note 46, *supra*.

[102] Though not part of this study, the experience at ETSI, which appears to have had no *ex ante* royalty disclosures since the adoption of its policy in 2007, supports this hypothesis.

[103] At IEEE, however, only 3% (n=11) of all patent disclosures contained royalty-free commitments. In this case, it is worth noting that IEEE provides a standardized form of Letter of Assurance in which most disclosers indicate that they are willing to license their patents on FRAND terms.

[104] For an explanation of these and other common FRAND licensing terms, *see* ABA Manual, *supra* note 8, at 49-67.

[105] Informal discussions with individuals who were involved in the development of the IEEE *ex ante* policy confirm that expressly permitting the disclosure of non-royalty licensing terms within the context of IEEE standards-development was a goal of the policy.

2.   *Attitudes Toward VITA Policy.* We surveyed VITA members regarding their general and specific views toward the licensing information solicited by VITA's *ex ante* policy. In general, a significant majority of respondents (83%, n=34) felt that the adoption of VITA's *ex ante* policy made standards development at VITA more open and transparent. Only 17% (n=7) noticed no change and none felt that the policy had made VITA less open or transparent. With respect to the specific information disclosed under the policy, 93% (n=39) of respondents felt that royalty information disclosed by patent holders was important to them when considering whether to approve a proposed VITA standard. When asked whether the disclosure of a relevant patent affected their desire to work on and approve a VITA standard, 43% (n=18) responded that it depends on the licensing terms, and 40% (n=17) responded that it depends on both the licensing terms and the patent holder. Based on these data, it appears that, at least among current VITA participants, the information disclosed under the *ex ante* disclosure policy is both desired and perceived to be a useful input to the standards-development process.

B.   *Number of Standards.*

We counted the number of independent standardization activities that were started, as well as the total number of standards that were approved, each year from 2004 and 2003, respectively, to 2010 at each of VITA, IEEE and IETF. The number of standards *approved* by an SDO is a relatively common measure of SDO performance. The significance of standards *starts* to SDO performance, however, is less well-understood.[106] We measured both the number of standards activities started and the number of standards ultimately approved at each SDO for several reasons. First, we sought to understand the effect of the VITA and IEEE *ex ante* policies on standardization processes within these organizations. In both organizations, it takes an average of three to five years from the introduction of a proposed standard until it is finally approved.[107] Thus, it is probable that very few standards started after the adoption of these policies would have been approved at the time of this study.[108] Second, we wanted to test whether SDO participants would, as predicted, begin to take standardization proposals elsewhere following the adoption of *ex ante* policies. If this were the case, one might expect standard starts to decrease following adoption of these policies, an effect that would be seen within the years immediately following policy adoption, and would not exhibit the time lag associated with standard approvals.

1.   *Standards Starts.*

Table B.1 shows the number of independent standards activities started at each SDO from 2004 to 2010.

---

[106] Thus, while an organization that starts many projects and finishes just a few might not be viewed as successful, an organization that starts just a few high-value projects and completes them all might be considered a great success. We address *quality* metrics in Section IV.C, *infra*, and in this Section focus exclusively on the *number* of standards processed by an SDO.

[107] *See* Section IV.B, *infra*.

[108] This fact suggests that further study may be appropriate in a few years time, after a substantial number of standards approved in a given year were started in 2007 or later.

Table B.1

Number of New Standards Activities (2004-2010)

	VITA	IEEE	IETF
Range	5-19	78-187	1085-1533
Std. deviation (σ)	5.44	40	153
Mean$_{2004\text{-}06}$	11.0	83	1317
Mean$_{2007\text{-}10}$	10.3	138	1346
Slope ($m_{2004\text{-}07}$)*	-0.24	0.04	0.14
Slope ($m_{2007\text{-}10}$)*	-0.04	0.26	0.19

* normalized to 1.0

Figure B.1.a shows the number of standards starts at VITA during this period.

Figure B.1.a

VITA Standards Activities Started by Year (2004-2010)

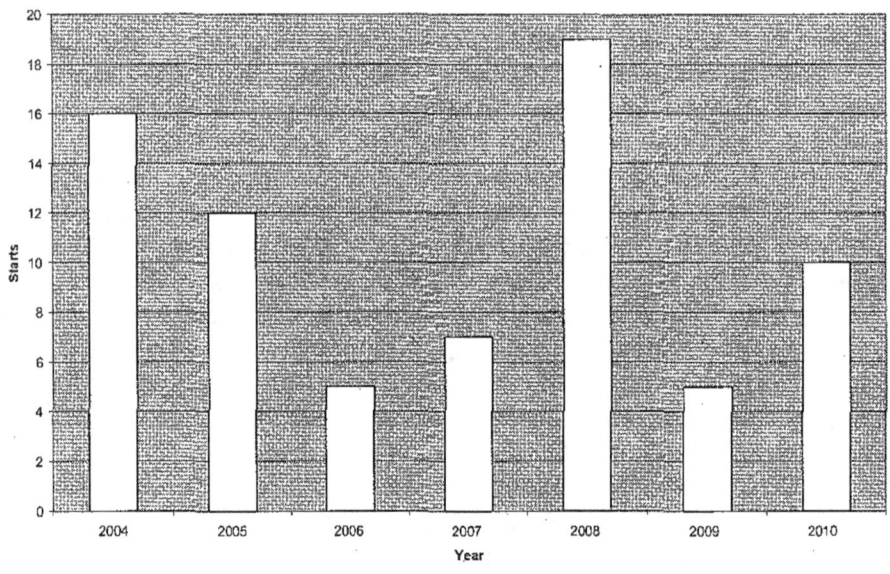

Figures B.1.b and B.1.c illustrate trends in the mean number of annual standards starts at each SDO both before and after 2007. For illustrative purposes, values are normalized to a scale of 1.0 in order to allow comparison of trends at SDOs of different sizes.

Figure B.1.b

Standards Activities Started by Year (2004-07)

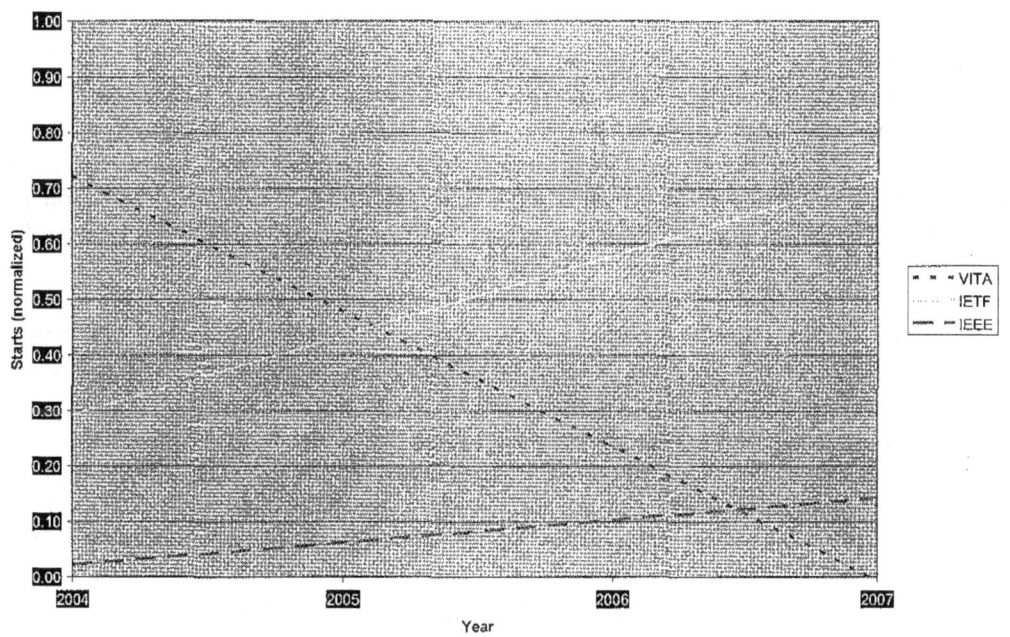

Figure B.1.c

Standards Activities Started by Year (2007-10)

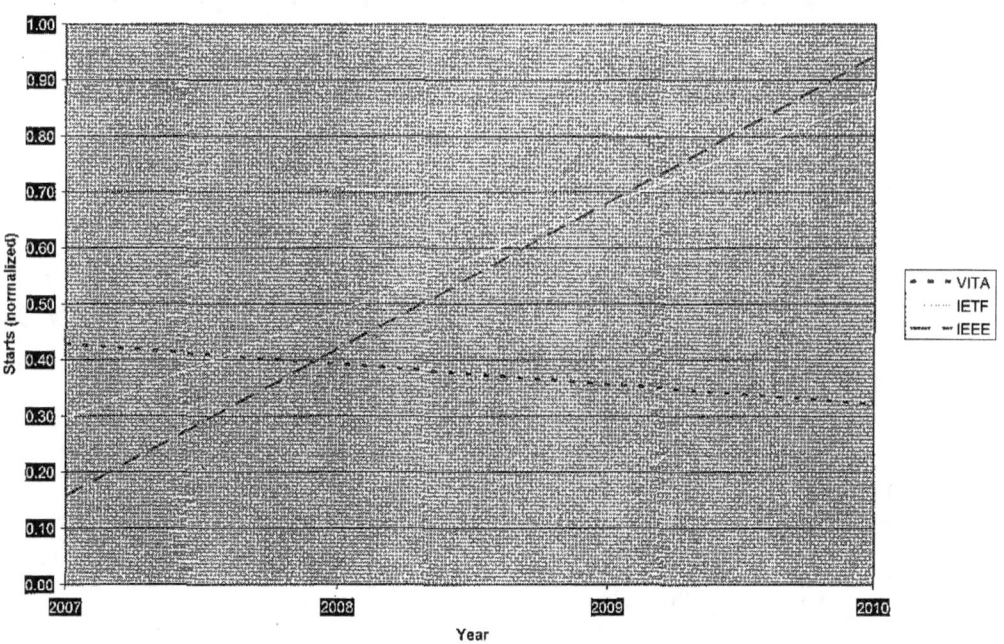

As illustrated in Figures B.1.b and B.1.c, IEEE experienced a relatively steady increase in standards started from 2004 to 2010, with a significantly sharper increase from 2007 to 2010 (m=1.32) than 2004 to 2007 (m=0.20). VITA experienced a significant net decline in standards starts from 2004 to 2007, and a more modest net decline in standards starts from 2007 to 2010, though performance in this later period was highly volatile and marked by both a significant increase in 2008, a corresponding decrease in 2009, and a modest gain in 2010. Normalized IETF data is presented for comparison and suggests that, at least from 2007 to 2010, there was a general industry trend toward greater numbers of standards starts (noting an almost identical trajectory for IETF and IEEE from 2007 to 2010).

Based on these data, we do not find a negative correlation between the adoption of *ex ante* policies at VITA and IEEE and the number of standards starts at these SDOs over this period. At IEEE, the trend following adoption of its *ex ante* policy is clearly upward, and while we would be hesitant to attribute this result to the adoption of an *ex ante* policy, it is clear that the negative predictions made by critics of *ex ante* policies did not come to pass at IEEE. At VITA, the pattern of standards starts following adoption of its *ex ante* policy is more volatile, but also suggests that the *ex ante* policy did not have a significant impact on the number of standards starts at the organization. In particular, during the period from 2007 to 2008, immediately after the *ex ante* policy was adopted, while VITA was embroiled in a heated exchange with Motorola over VITA's ANSI re-accreditation,[109] VITA saw the highest number of standards starts during the period. Had VITA's *ex ante* policy, or the issues surrounding its adoption, been a significant concern to VITA members, one might expect them to defer starting new standardization projects within VITA. The result, however, was precisely the opposite. The fact that standards starts dropped significantly at VITA in 2009 could have numerous causes (as could the increase in standards starts in 2008), but in neither case does the adoption of VITA's *ex ante* policy seem to have been a significant factor.

2. *Standards Approved.* Table B.2 shows the number of standards approved at each SDO from 2003 to 2010.

Table B.2
Number of Standards Approved, by Year (2003-2010)

	VITA	IEEE	IETF
Range	0-8	61-101	262-343
Std. deviation (σ)	2.5	11	28
Mean$_{2003-06}$	2.25	75	786
Mean$_{2007-10}$	4.50	83	935
Slope ($m_{2003-07}$)*	-0.05	0.06	0.13
Slope ($m_{2007-10}$)*	0.25	0.18	0.14

* normalized to 1.0

---

[109] *See* notes 42-43, *supra*, and accompanying text.

Figures B.2.a and B.2.b show the trends in mean number of annual standards approvals at each SDO both before and after 2007. For illustrative purposes, values are normalized to a scale of 1.0 in order to allow comparison of trends at SDOs of different sizes.

Figure B.2.a

Standards Approved by Year (2003-07)

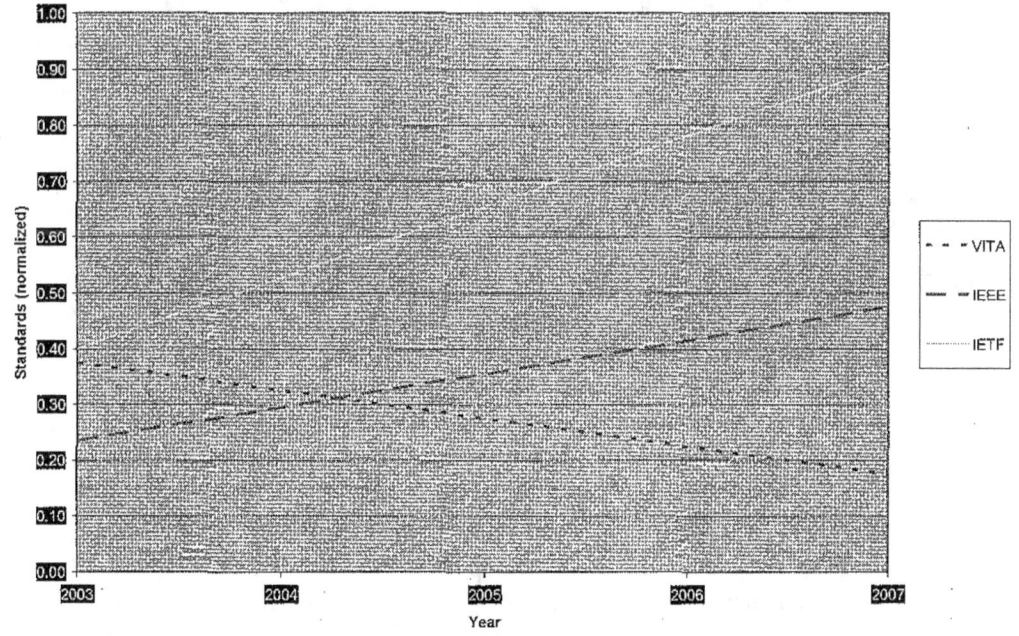

Figure B.2.b

Standards Approved by Year (2007-10)

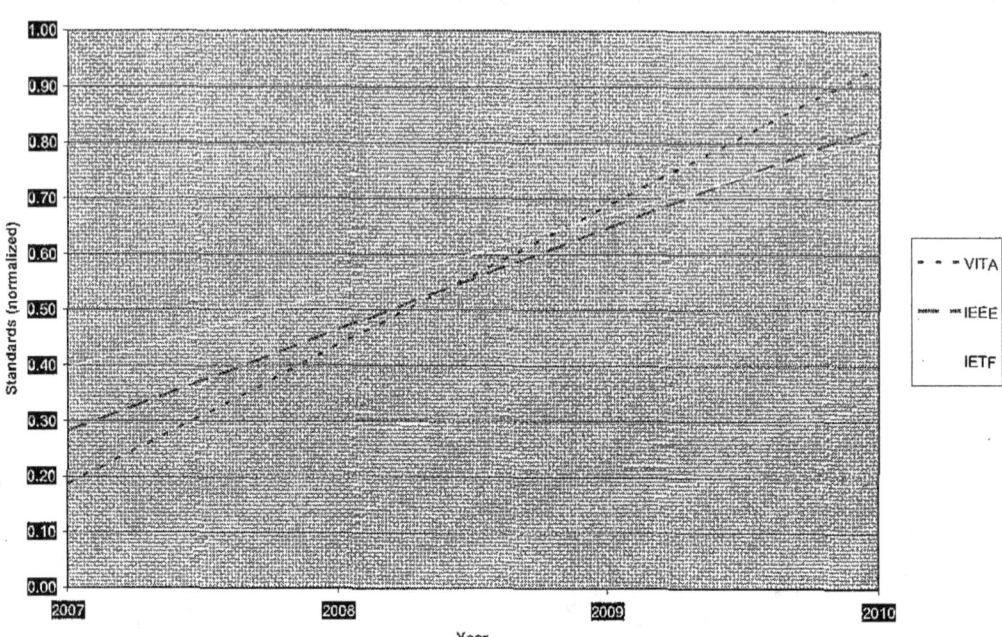

As illustrated in Figures B.2.a and B.2.b, VITA experienced a decline in standards adopted from 2003 to 2007 (m=-2.20) and a steep increase from 2007 to 2010 (m=3.81). IEEE experienced increases in standards adopted during both periods, but the rate of increase after 2007 was significantly greater (m_{03-06}=2.72, m_{07-10}=3.47). Thus, it seems clear that the adoption of *ex ante* policies by these SDOs did not result in a decrease in the number of standards adopted.

However, as suggested by the trend line for IETF, there appears to have been a general increase in the number of standards approved elsewhere in the industry from 2007 to 2010, with all three SDOs achieving near their maximum approval level in 2010. Thus, while it appears that the adoption of *ex ante* policies did not cause a *decline* in the number of standards approved by VITA or IEEE from 2007 to 2010, the converse conclusion (that the adoption of an *ex ante* policy contributed to the *increase* in standards approved) cannot reasonably be drawn in view of general industry trends over this period.

3.   *Conclusions.* Based on the data reviewed, we did not find evidence of a causal connection between the adoption of *ex ante* policies at VITA or IEEE and a decrease in either standards activities started or standards approved. Rather, with respect to standards starts, VITA experienced a steep increase in the year immediately following the adoption of its *ex ante* policy, followed by an equally steep drop the next year, with an overall increase during the period studied, and IEEE experienced a steady upward trend throughout the period studied. With respect to standards approved, both VITA and IEEE experienced significant increases following adoption of their *ex ante* policies,

which closely tracks overall trends in the industry as exemplified by IETF, suggesting that factors other than *ex ante* policy adoption were largely responsible for effects observed.

C.   *Length of Standardization Process.*

1.   *Historical Data.* Numerous commentators have noted the lengthy time periods required to develop consensus standards in the ICT sector.[110] Farrell cites several examples from the 1980s and 1990s in which average time requirements for standardization at SDOs such as IEEE, IEC and ISO ranged from five to seven years.[111] Simcoe measured increases in the time required for standardization at IETF from 1992 and 2000 and found a 177% increase over the period (from an average of 192 days to 549 days).[112] He explored three possible explanations for this significant increase in standardization time: greater technical complexity of IETF standards, growth of the IETF organization itself, and a rise in internal conflicts among committees and working groups within IETF.[113] Interestingly, Simcoe found statistically significant correlations between several of these factors and the lengthening of the standardization process at IETF, but *intellectual property* disclosures made at IETF "had no measurable impact on average duration of the standard setting process."[114]

Against this backdrop, we measured the number of days elapsed between the introduction of a draft standard and approval of the corresponding final standard at VITA, IEEE and IETF from 2003 to 2010. The results are summarized in Table C.1 below.

---

[110] In most cases, the protracted length of standardization processes is viewed unfavorably. However, some commentators have questioned whether a shorter time to standardization is always beneficial. Shah and Kesan, for example, observe, based on regression analysis of standardization duration and impact, that "there appears to be no relationship between a longer development process and the ultimate impact of a standard." Rajiv C. Shah & Jay P. Kesan, *An Empirical Examination of Open Standards Development* (U. Ill L. & Econ. Research Papers Series, Research Paper No. LE07-039) at 21 (2007) (available at http://papers.ssrn.com/sol3/papers.cfm?abstract_id=1031749). Thus, while Shah and Kesan support reforms intended to decrease the time required for standardization, they do not feel that such reforms will result in standards of higher impact. Froomkin has lauded the IETF's open and participatory processes, particularly its enablement of vigorous and substantive multilateral debate; from this perspective, greater speed would reduce the deliberative power of such an organization. A. Michael Froomkin, *Habermas@Discourse.net: Toward a Critical Theory of Cyberspace*, 116 HARV. L. REV. 749, 783 (2003). Thus, while market participants may be driven by the desire to standardize products as rapidly as possible, it is not uniformly agreed that acceleration of the standardization process would increase overall welfare.

[111] Joseph Farrell, *Choosing the Rules for Formal Standardization* at 7 (working paper, U.C. Berkeley, Dept. Economics 1996) (available at http://citeseerx.ist.psu.edu/viewdoc/download?doi=10.1.1.73.6537&rep=rep1&type=pdf).

[112] Simcoe, *supra* note 86, at 16 (measuring the "elapsed time between publication of the initial and final versions of an Internet Draft").

[113] *Id.* at 16.

[114] *Id.* at 23.

Table C.1
Average Time (in days) for Standard Approval (2003-2010)

	VITA	IEEE	IETF
Range	379-1542	1342-1630	694-966
Std. deviation (σ)	371	108	100
Mean$_{2003\text{-}06}$	979	1525	786
Mean$_{2007\text{-}10}$	1298	1498	935
Slope ($m_{2003\text{-}07}$)	33	65	54
Slope ($m_{2007\text{-}10}$)	2	-39	8

For IETF, these data show a steady increase in the length of time required for standardization, from 694 to 925 days, an increase of 33.2%. While this increase is substantial, it is far lower than the 177% increase that Simcoe observed at IETF from 1992-2000. And while the average time for standardization at IETF was higher from 2007 to 2010 (935 days) than from 2003 to 2006 (786 days), the rate of increase (slope (m)) decreased from 54 to 8 from the earlier period to the later (a decline of 84%). This data suggests that an upward trend for standardization timing may still exist in the ICT industry, but may not be accelerating as rapidly as it did during the 1990s.

At IEEE, in contrast, the observed trend is downward. Average time for standardization during the period from 2003 to 2006 was 1,525 days, while average time during the period from 2007 to 2010 was only 1,498 days (a decrease of 27 days, or 1.7%). At VITA (σ=371), fluctuations from year to year are more pronounced than at IETF (σ=100) and IEEE (σ=108) due to the smaller number of standards under development at VITA at any given time. And while the average time for approval of VITA standards approved from 2007 to 2010 was 1,298 days, as opposed to 979 days for the period from 2003 to 2006 (an increase of 33%), the *rate* of increase declined by 93% ($m_{03\text{-}06}$ = 33; $m_{07\text{-}10}$ = 2), which is greater than the 84% decline in the rate of increase seen at IETF, which has no *ex ante* policy. Thus it is unlikely that the adoption of VITA's *ex ante* policy can be shown to have caused a lengthening of the standardization process at VITA, at least given the data available today.

This conclusion is consistent with Simcoe's finding that there was no correlation between intellectual property disclosures at IETF and lengthening of the standardization process.[115] Rather, it is possible that the continued lengthening of the VITA standardization process, which tracks the overall lengthening in the industry, exemplified by IETF, may be attributable to the other factors identified by Simcoe, such as growth in membership, increasing technical complexity and a rise in internal (non-patent) conflicts and competition among participants.[116] One caveat that should be mentioned is that most of the standards approved by VITA from 2007 to 2010 were actually started *before* adoption of VITA's *ex ante* policy. It will be some years before a sufficient quantity of

---

[115] *Id.* It should be noted, however, that the disclosures studied by Simcoe were *ex ante patent* disclosures, not *ex ante licensing* disclosures, making the extension of his findings to the current study imperfect.
[116] Simcoe, *supra* note 86, at 16.

approved VITA standards that were started *after* adoption of the *ex ante* policy can be studied in detail.

2. *Survey Data - Perceptions.* To supplement the historical data discussed above, we asked VITA survey respondents to report their perceptions of the effect of the adoption of VITA's *ex ante* policy on the overall speed of standardization at VITA. The responses are summarized in Table C.2 below.

Table C.2
VITA Survey Data: Standardization Speed

Effect of VITA *ex ante* Policy on Standardization Speed	Compared to VITA pre-*ex ante* (n=43)	Compared to Other SDOs (n=44)
Faster	18%	20%
No effect	33%	36%
Slower	2%	2%
Don't Know	21%	18%
Lacks Basis for Comparison[117]	26%	23%

These responses are notable in that, as discussed above, the mean time for standardization at VITA increased following adoption of the *ex ante* policy. Yet the perception of a meaningful fraction of VITA participants (18%) was that standardization at VITA actually became *faster* after its adoption of the *ex ante* policy, and only a single respondent believed that standardization at VITA had become slower. Moreover, there is a significant association (p=0.0004) between experience with VITA and views regarding the speed of standardization at VITA: of the group responding that standardization at VITA became faster or did not change following adoption of the *ex ante* policy (n=22), 46% had at least ten years experience with VITA and 68% had five or more years experience with the organization. Conversely, of the respondents who said that they did not know or had no basis for comparison, 89% and 91% respectively had two or fewer years experience with VITA. Likewise, there was marginally significant (p=0.0499) evidence to suggest that the more SDOs a respondent actively participated in, the more likely he or she was to believe that *ex ante* disclosure of licensing terms makes the standardization process at VITA faster than at other SDOs. And among individuals who reported that they actually check *ex ante* licensing disclosures at VITA (n=22), 77% believed that the speed of standardization at VITA was unchanged or became faster at VITA after adoption of the *ex ante* policy, and 73% believed that the speed of standardization at VITA was the same or faster than at other SDOs.[118]

---

[117] The respondent either did not participate in VITA prior to adoption of the *ex ante* policy in 2007 or does not participate in other SDOs, as applicable.

[118] There was a statistically significant correlation between whether one checked *ex ante* licensing disclosures and his or her views regarding both the speed of standardization at VITA before and after adoption of the *ex ante* policy (p=0.0055), and as compared to other SDOs (p=0.0396). Those who reported that they did not check disclosures generally seemed to be newer to, and less familiar with, the organization, and of those not checking disclosures, 65% (n=13) expressed no opinion regarding the effect of the *ex ante* policy on the comparative speed of standardization at VITA, and 74% (n=14) expressed no

Thus, it appears that among VITA participants having greater experience with the organization or SDOs in general, and among participants that are familiar enough with the organization's procedures to check for *ex ante* licensing disclosures, there is a general feeling that the adoption of VITA's *ex ante* policy did not result in a lengthening of the standardization process. How can this be reconciled with the observed lengthening of the average time to standardization at VITA in the years following adoption of the *ex ante* policy? One possible explanation is that "veteran" participants *have* observed the acceleration of some standardization processes at VITA, or at least portions of those processes. The fact that overall standardization time has continued to increase may be attributable not to the *ex ante* policy, but to other factors such as increasing technical complexity and length of standards, both of which have been observed by Simcoe in his study of IETF.[119] If this is the case, then it is not surprising that veteran standards developers may have observed a streamlining of certain aspects of the standardization process (i.e., those associated with patent and royalty uncertainty) and responded accordingly, even while overall standardization time has increased for unrelated reasons.

3. *Response to Disclosures.* Critics have predicted that *ex ante* policies are likely to result in multiple rounds of license negotiation between patent holders and implementers, thus lengthening the standards development process and delaying approval of standards. As discussed in Section IV.G.1 below, we have identified only one instance in which a disagreement over licensing terms initiated after an *ex ante* disclosure at VITA resulted in the amendment of the proposed license agreement disclosed by the patent holder. In addition, as shown in Table G.1 below, the actions taken by VITA members in response to a disclosed royalty that they deemed "too high" varied in terms of their potential to delay standardization by any significant amount. Some actions, such as raising the issue at a meeting or contacting the patent holder, have a low potential for delay, while others, such as attempting to alter the technical design to avoid the patent claims or blocking development or approval pending a resolution of the issue, have a greater potential for delay. It is interesting to note, however, that only a fraction of VITA respondents (13%, n=6) indicated that they had taken measures likely to delay standardization in response to a royalty disclosure. Most respondents took no action at all. While these results are not necessarily dispositive (a single determined participant can sometimes delay progress to a disproportionate degree), they do suggest that VITA's *ex ante* policy has not caused a significant number of VITA respondents to engage in activity that would be likely to cause material delays in standardization.

4. *Conclusions.* Though the data relating to length of the standardization process at VITA and IEEE is complex, we do not believe the data suggests a correlation between the adoption of *ex ante* policies at these organizations and an increase in standardization time. At IEEE, standardization time decreased over the period from 2007-2010. At VITA, based on highly divergent annual averages, standardization time

---

opinion regarding the effect of the *ex ante* policy on the speed of standardization at VITA as compared to other SDOs.

[119] Simcoe, *supra* note 86. We did not measure length or complexity of standards documents nor correlate this variable against time to approval. Such an analysis would be of potential interest for a future study.

increased modestly over this period, but at a slower rate of increase than the immediately preceding period (2004-2007) and a slower rate than at IETF. Moreover, more than half of VITA survey respondents perceived that standardization speed at VITA had either accelerated or remained the same following adoption of the *ex ante* policy, with such responses correlated to the length of the respondent's experience with VITA. Finally, an analysis of the actual measures taken by VITA participants in response to *ex ante* royalty disclosures shows that few participated in tactics likely to delay standardization at VITA.

D.   *Personal Time Commitment.*

Table D.1 shows survey responses relating to changes in VITA respondents' personal time spent on standardization activities after the adoption of VITA's *ex ante* policy, both as compared to VITA prior to the adoption of the policy and to other SDOs.

Table D.1
VITA Survey Data: Personal Time Commitment

Time that Respondent spent on VITA standards activities	(a) Compared to VITA pre-*ex ante* (n=43)	(b) Compared to Other SDOs (n=44)
Less time	12%	7%
No effect	33%	43%
More time	7%	9%
Don't Know	23%	20%
Lacks Basis for Comparison[120]	26%	20%

Unlike the responses relating to overall speed of standardization at VITA (see Section IV.C above), the number of respondents stating that their personal time commitments to VITA had changed following adoption of the *ex ante* policy, either positively or negatively, were similar and, in each case, relatively small. Most respondents (82% in column (a) and 83% in column (b)), indicated no change in time commitment, or that they did not know or lacked a basis for comparison. As with overall speed of standardization, however, there was a strong statistical correlation (p=0.0002) between responses and experience with VITA: of the group responding that their personal time commitment to VITA *decreased* following adoption of the *ex ante* policy (n=5), 80% had five or more years experience with the organization and of those who responded that their personal time commitment to VITA did not change (n=14), 50% had ten or more years experience with VITA and 71% had five or more years experience with the organization.

To investigate the extent to which changes in personal time commitment might be attributable to the adoption of VITA's *ex ante* policy, we also asked respondents a

---

[120] The respondent either did not participate in VITA prior to adoption of the *ex ante* policy in 2007 or does not participate in other SDOs, as applicable.

number of questions intended to assess the level of new activity required by the policy. First, we asked whether participants checked *ex ante* licensing disclosures when a new standard is proposed at VITA,[121] on the ground that those who did not check disclosures would be unlikely to have increased activity as a result of such disclosures. 51% (n=23) of respondents said that they checked such licensing disclosures, and 57% of those responding positively (n=13) said they checked either "always" or "frequently". It is among this group that we would expect to see increased time commitments associated with VITA. Yet of those VITA participants who said they checked licensing disclosures "always" or "frequently", only one (8%) said that he or she was required to spend more time on VITA following the adoption of its *ex ante* policy, and 67% (n=8) said that they devoted the same or less time to VITA standards activities.[122]

Thus, as with overall standardization speed, among VITA participants having greater experience with the organization or SDOs in general, and among participants that are familiar enough with the organization's procedures to check for *ex ante* licensing disclosures, there appears to be a general sense that the adoption of VITA's *ex ante* policy did not result in an increased individual time commitment.

E. *Membership*.

1. *VITA Membership Fluctuations, 2004-2010.* Table E.1 below shows the year-over-year membership changes in VITA from 2004 to 2010, based on the methodology described in Section III.B.3.e above:

Table E.1
Changes in VITA Membership (2004 to 2010)

Year	Members Departing from Prior Year	Members Added from Prior Year	Net Change
2004	baseline	baseline	baseline
2005	5	20	+15
2006	14	29	+15
2007	16	8	-8
2008	22	22	0
2009	8	6	-2
2010	21	42	21
Mean	14.3	21.2	6.8

---

[121] In a separate question, we also asked whether respondents checked patent disclosures. Responses were comparable as to these two questions.

[122] In general, we found a statistically significant correlation (p=0.0339) between whether one checked *ex ante* licensing disclosures and the impact on his or her time commitment to VITA. Those who reported that they did not check disclosures generally seemed to be newer to, and less familiar with, the organization, and 74% (n=14) of those not checking expressed no opinion regarding the effect of the *ex ante* policy on their individual time commitment to the organization.

VITA adopted its *ex ante* policy in January 2007. In that year, VITA gained eight new members and lost 16 members, resulting in a net loss of eight members. Membership remained relatively stable in 2008 and 2009, with a significant increase (a net gain of 21 members) in 2010.[123] Thus, over the period from 2007 to 2010, VITA saw a significant net increase in members, and if any membership decline was caused by the adoption of VITA's *ex ante* policy, it would have been the short-term net loss of members in 2007. However, the evidence discussed below suggests that the *ex ante* policy did not result even in the 2007 net membership decline experienced by VITA.

2. *Little Public Opposition to VITA ex ante Policy.* Of the 16 members who left VITA in 2007, only one (Motorola) publicly opposed VITA's *ex ante* policy. The VITA VSO membership approved the VITA *ex ante* policy in January 2007 by a vote of 35-2 with 12 abstentions.[124] Presumably, a member that voted in favor of the policy would not have withdrawn from the organization due to the adoption of the policy. Thus, while it is clear that the *ex ante* policy was a major factor in Motorola's resignation from the organization,[125] we found no evidence that any other VITA member publicly opposed the adoption of the *ex ante* policy.

3. *General Membership Fluctuations at VITA.* Of the 16 members that withdrew from VITA in 2007, at least four rejoined the organization in a subsequent year. This effect is not unusual, as VITA membership fluctuates significantly from year to year as work on standards of interest to particular members is commenced or concluded. Other departures annually are due to changing business priorities, failure of smaller firms, and acquisitions by non-members. Based on information gathered during an interview with VITA's executive director, each 2007 departure other than Motorola's can be attributed to one of these other causes. As shown in Table E.1, VITA experienced an average loss of 14.3 members per year between 2004 and 2010 (offset by an average annual gain of 21.2 members, for an average net gain of 6.8 members). Thus, the loss of 16 members in 2007 is only slightly above VITA's average annual membership loss.[126]

---

[123] There is no indication that VITA membership has dropped significantly as of May 22, 2011.

[124] The vote was taken at a meeting of the VSO held in Long Beach, California at which there were 51 eligible voting representatives. See Letter to VSO Attendees dated Nov. 16, 2006 (available at http://www.vita.com/disclosure/vso-voting-ex-ante.pdf). Note that only VITA members that are active in VSO standardization activities are eligible to vote on VSO matters.

[125] *See* notes 42-43, *supra*, and accompanying text. It has been reported that after withdrawing from VITA, Motorola sold the division that had participated in VITA to Emerson, another non-member. Lindsay, *supra* note 24, at 7, n.22.

[126] VITA's membership ranges from very large, multinational enterprises to small businesses. VITA's current members include, for example, large enterprises and patent holders such as General Electric, Agilent Technologies, BAE Systems, Boeing, General Dynamics, MIT Lincoln Laboratories, Tyco Electronics and Xilinx. While we did not attempt to weight VITA membership departures and additions by size, patent holdings or any other factor, we did not notice any significant trend toward larger or smaller members departing or joining VITA during the period studied. In future studies, it might be desirable to investigate whether any connection exists between departing or joining an SDO based on size of the company and/or the standards-relevant patent portfolio.

4.   *Comparison to IETF Attendance.* Figures E.4.a and E.4.b below enable a comparison of the trends in VITA's membership versus IETF's North American meeting attendance over the period from 2004 to 2010.

Figure E.4.a

VITA Membership Changes by Year

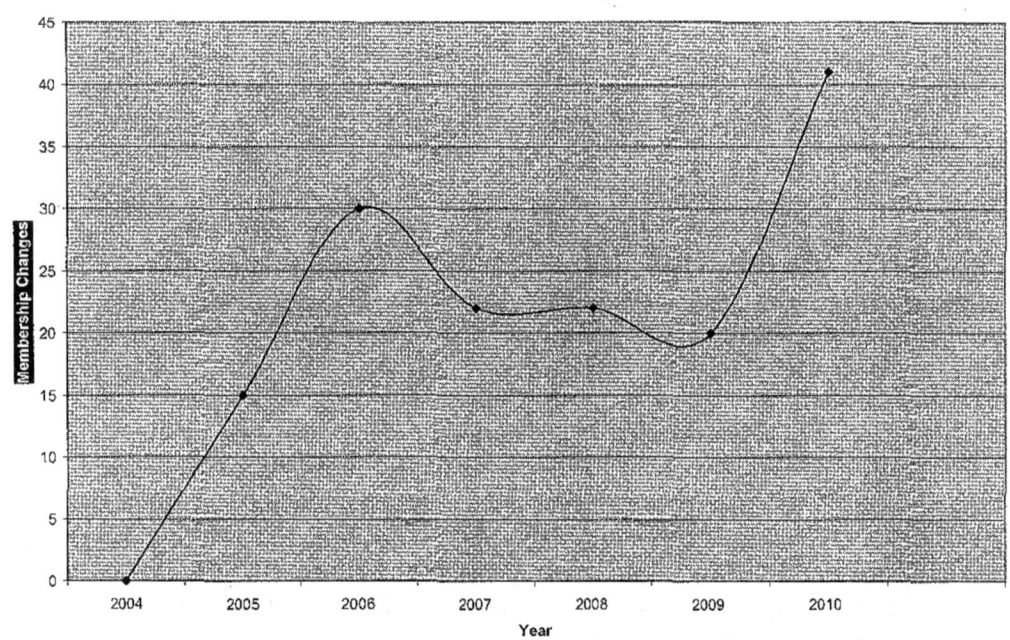

IETF N. American Attendance Changes by Year (2004 Baseline)

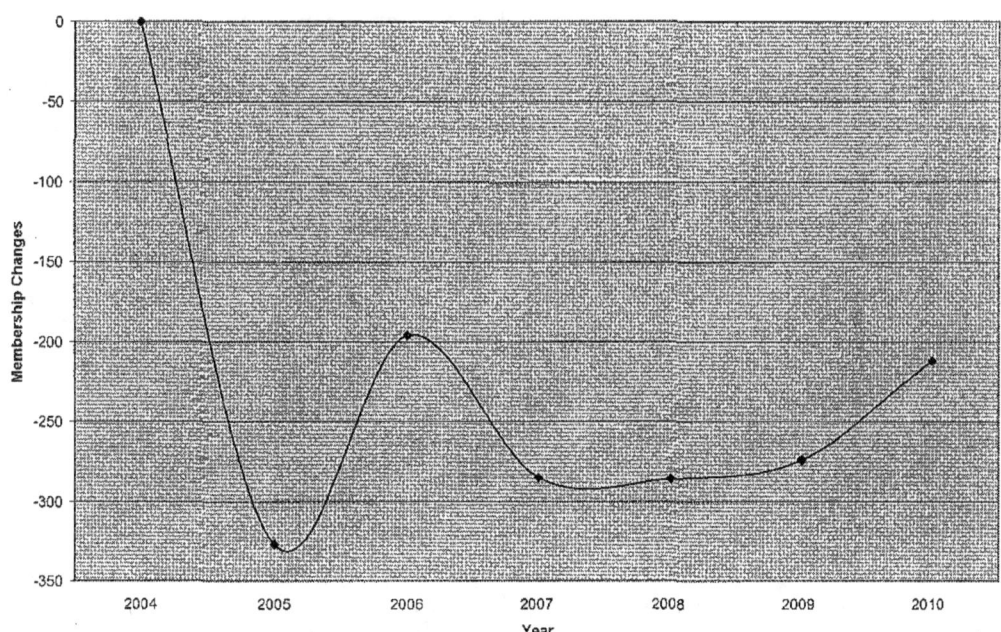

As shown in Figures E.4.a and E.4.b, beginning in 2005, the general trend in IETF attendance tracks VITA membership changes over the same period. Like VITA, IETF experienced a material increase in attendance in 2006, a drop in attendance in 2007, relatively steady attendance in 2008 and 2009, and an increase in 2010. While it is difficult to draw precise comparisons between VITA membership and IETF attendance, it is informative that the general participation trends in both organizations are comparable over most of the period studied, further suggesting that the membership drop experienced by VITA in 2007 may have been attributable to general industry conditions rather than its adoption of an *ex ante* policy.

     5.   *Survey Data*. We surveyed VITA participants regarding their employers' reactions to VITA's adoption of an *ex ante* policy. 74% of respondents (n=31) stated that their employer did not consider withdrawing from VITA as a result of its adoption of an *ex ante* policy, and only 7% (n=3) said their employer did consider withdrawing[127] (19% did not know). Moreover, when respondents were asked, all other things being equal, whether they would recommend that their employer join another SDO with an *ex ante* policy similar to VITA's, 56% (n=23) said they would either strongly or moderately recommend such an action, 44% said they would neither recommend nor discourage such

---

[127] There is a significant association (p=0.0027) between reporting that a participant's employer had previously submitted a patent disclosure to an SDO and that employer's consideration of withdrawal from VITA as a result of the adoption of its *ex ante* policy. However, due to the small number of respondents reporting that their employers had considered withdrawing from VITA (n=3), no conclusions about trend can be drawn from this sample.

an action and none said that they would discourage it. Based on these responses, it is reasonable to conclude that VITA's *ex ante* policy is supported by its current membership and had little effect on VITA membership beyond the known opposition and withdrawal of Motorola. We acknowledge, however, that a sampling bias may be present with respect to these responses, as any members who withdrew from the organization based on dissatisfaction with the *ex ante* policy would not be part of the pool of current VITA members surveyed.[128]

6.   *Conclusions.* VITA membership has increased since the adoption of its *ex ante* policy in 2007, despite a slightly above-average net decrease in members that year. The data we reviewed does not suggest that the adoption of VITA's *ex ante* policy caused the departure of more than one member from VITA. Overall, VITA's membership trends from 2005 to 2010 have tracked closely with industry averages as exemplified by IETF.

F.   *Quality of Standards.*

Measuring the "quality" of technical standards is inherently difficult, imprecise and subjective. Thus, in order to make an assessment of the change in quality, if any, of standards following the adoption of *ex ante* policies, we measured three different variables: quality perceptions by VITA participants, external recognition of VITA standards and impact based on citation data derived from search engine hits.[129]

1.   *Survey Data.* We surveyed VITA members to determine their views regarding the effect, if any, that the adoption of VITA's *ex ante* policy had on their perceptions of the quality of VITA standards. As shown in Table F.1, 79% of respondents felt that adoption of VITA's *ex ante* policy improved the quality of VITA standards. Moreover, among participants having ten or more years of experience with VITA (n=11), 90% responded that adoption of VITA's *ex ante* policy made the quality of VITA standards "much better" or "somewhat better".

---

[128] To this end, it has been suggested that a fruitful avenue for future research may be the polling of former VITA members.

[129] Other methods of assessing the impact of standards have been proposed. For example, Rysman and Simcoe have suggested that SDO performance can be measured by the number of patent documents citing patents disclosed to the SDO. Marc Rysman & Tim Simcoe, *Patents and the Performance of Voluntary Standard Setting Organizations*, 54 MANAGEMENT SCI. 1920 (2008) (studying patent disclosures made at IEEE, IETF, the European Telecommunications Standards Institute (ETSI) and the International Telecommunications Union (ITU)). We elected not to use this approach, as it does not address the impact of standards as to which no patent disclosures have been made.

Table F.1
VITA Survey Data: Standards Quality

VITA's *ex ante* makes the quality of VITA standards	Percentage (n=43)
Much Better	53%
Somewhat Better	26%
No Difference	2%
Somewhat Worse	2%
Much Worse	0%
Don't Know	17%

We acknowledge, of course, that the responses of VITA participants with significant personal investments of time and effort in VITA standards development may reflect personal bias regarding the quality of VITA standards. Thus, future studies may benefit from obtaining views of more impartial observers in assessing the perceived quality of SDO standards.

2. *External Recognition.* External accolades and awards can also serve as measures of a standard's quality. One prominent electronics industry award is made by *Electronic Design* magazine, which each year chooses products and designs for its "Best Electronic Design" awards in numerous categories. In 2009, VITA Standards 66 and 67[130] were awarded Best Electronic Design awards in the Military & Aerospace category,[131] and in 2010, VITA Standard 65 ("VPX System Specifications and Practices") received the same award.[132] Prior to 2009, VITA had not won any significant industry awards. This recognition, and the development of the recognized standards, occurred after the adoption of VITA's *ex ante* policy, and evidences recent industry recognition of VITA's standards. Patent disclosures have not been made with respect to any of the recognized standards. Thus, while such industry awards to some degree validate the quality of VITA's technical program, a link with the *ex ante* policy is difficult to establish. At a minimum, the fact that VITA standards have won recent industry awards does tend to refute arguments that overall technical quality at an SDO adopting an *ex ante* policy will invariably suffer.

3. *Citation Data.* One method suggested by Shah and Kesan for assessing the relative value a technical standard is comparing the number of "hits" returned by

---

[130] Interestingly, neither of these standards had been formally approved by VITA at the time the award was made, and still had not been approved by May 2011. Nevertheless, products implementing these draft standards existed in the market and were viewed by the editors as sufficiently innovative to merit an award.

[131] Electronic Design Press Release, *Electronic Design* Announces 2009 Best Electronic Design Awards, Jan. 9, 2010 (available at
http://electronicdesign.com/article/services/electronic_design_announces_2009_best_electronic_design_award_winners_.aspx).

[132] VITA Press Release, OpenVPX Wins Electronic Design's Best Electronic Design Award, Dec. 10, 2010 (available at http://www.vita.com/news/VITA-NR-2010-
12%20OpenVPX%20Wins%20Best%20Electronic%20Design%20Award.pdf).

Internet search engines based on key words identifying one standard versus another.[133] Google hits may serve as indicators of a standard's "impact," as they reflect the number of articles referencing the standard, products that advertise compliance with the standard and discussions of the standard in technical groups.[134] While search engines such as Google invariably return results that are spurious in addition to those that are relevant, a comparison of hit ratios for different standards can shed light on the *relative* impact of such standards, the absolute number of hits being less informative.

Figure F.2 below is a plot of the thirty-four VITA standards adopted between 2003 and 2010 against the number of Google hits returned for each such standard, using the search methodology described in Section III.B.3.f above.

Figure F.2

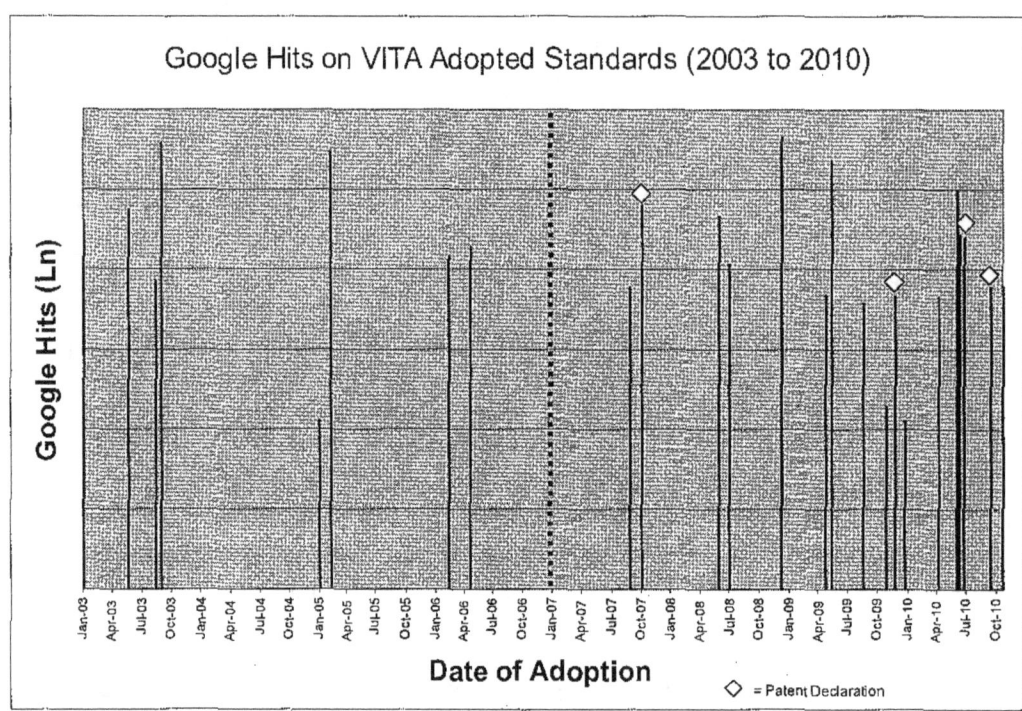

<hr />

[133] Rajiv C. Shah & Jay P. Kesan, *Open Standards and the Role of Politics*, PROC. 8TH ANN. INTL. DIGITAL GOVT. RESEARCH CONF. (2007) (finding that Google hits were "the best indicator of the impact of an open standard"). Google hits have also been used in various other fields to assess impact. *See, e.g.*, James P. Bagrow & Daniel ben-Avraham, *On the Google-Fame of Scientists and Other Populations*, 779 AIP CONF. PROC.: MODELING COOPERATIVE BEHAVIOR IN THE SOCIAL SCIENCES 81 (2005), Preslav Nakov & Marti Hearst, *A Study of Using Search Engine Page Hits as a Proxy for n-gram Frequencies*, PROCEEDINGS: RECENT ADVANCES IN NATURAL LANGUAGE PROCESSING (2005) and Su Cheng, et al., *PageRank, HITS and Impact Factor for Journal Ranking*, 6 COMP. SCI. & INFO. ENG. 285 (2009). Shah and Kesan have also utilized hits from Yahoo! and Google Scholar, citations in other standards and patent citations in assessing the impact of open standards. Shah & Kesan, *supra* note 110, at 7-9.

[134] It is not certain, of course, whether such discussions are favorable or unfavorable to the standard, and standards that are heavily criticized could garner as many or more hits than standards that are uniformly praised.

Range: <100 to 81,300

The number of hits per standard ranged from 81,300 hits for VITA 42.0 "XMC" to fewer than 100 hits for several standards.[135] The average number of hits for a VITA standard in this sample was 11,184, with standard deviation (after logarithmic transformation) of 2.06. The data are not markedly different if the time period examined is split at the point that VITA's *ex ante* policy was adopted in January 2007. Thus, the average number of hits for the thirteen VITA standards approved prior to January 2007 was 12,856, and the average number of hits for the twenty-one VITA standards approved after January 2007 was 10,149.[136] Moreover, the number of standards in each sub-period that exceeded the average number of hits for the full period was nearly identical: 3 of 13 (23.1%) for pre-2007 standards and 5 of 21 (23.8%) for post-2007 standards. Thus, it appears that the adoption of VITA's *ex ante* policy, *per se*, did not have a discernable impact on the number of hits per VITA standard.

We also examined the number of hits associated with approved VITA standards as to which *ex ante* licensing disclosures had been made. These standards are noted in Figure F.1. Among the twenty-one VITA standards approved from 2007 to 2010, the standards as to which disclosures were made ranked 4th, 8th, 11th and 15th in terms of Google hits, a relatively even distribution suggesting that the presence of *ex ante* licensing disclosures did not have a material effect on these standards' impact.

4.   *Conclusions.* A significant majority of survey respondents, and nearly all respondents having 10 or more years experience with VITA, believed that the adoption of the *ex ante* policy improved the overall quality of VITA standards. VITA standards garnered two external industry awards after 2007. Finally, based on an analysis of search engine hits on VITA standards approved since 2004, we did not detect significant differences between the impact of VITA standards before and after adoption of the *ex ante* policy. Thus, we do not find evidence that the quality of VITA standards deteriorated following adoption of its *ex ante* policy, and find some evidence suggesting that quality improved.

---

[135] Interestingly, contrary to common intuition, older standards did not consistently yield more hits than newer standards. In fact, VITA 42.0, which received 81,300 hits, was approved in 2008, while VITA 1.0-1994 "VME64", which was approved in 1994, received only slightly more, at 88,500. Moreover, the fact that several VITA standards with approval dates ranging from 2005 to 2010 yielded fewer than 100 hits suggests both that very low hit rates are not caused simply by the recentness of a standard's approval and, more importantly, that Google is not returning large quantities of spurious results in response to search queries for these standards.

The distribution of the present data set is consistent with the power law distribution that Shah and Kesan observed in a study of 634 IETF standards approved between 2000 and 2003. Shah & Kesan, *supra* note 110, at 2. In Shah's and Kesan's study, 20% of Google hits were attributable to the 0.9% highest-ranking standards, and 80% of Google hits were attributable to the 17.5% highest-ranking standards. In our VITA data set, 20% of Google hits were attributable to the single highest-ranking standard (2.9% of the total sample), and 80% of Google hits were attributable to the 20.6% highest-ranking standards.

[136] The standard deviation of the pre-*ex ante* logarithmic data set is 2.21, whereas the standard deviation for the post-*ex ante* data set is 2.03, indicating that the post-2007 data set, perhaps because of its larger size, is somewhat more stable than the earlier data set.

G.   *Effect on Royalty Rates*.

Critics have predicted that *ex ante* policies will enable implementers of standards, either expressly or implicitly, to apply inappropriate pressure to patent holders to lower their royalty rates below fair or reasonable levels, and in some cases all the way to zero.[137] While we did not have access to information regarding the royalties charged by patent holders to individual licensees, we can make several observations regarding this prediction based on the data that we collected.

1.   *Royalty-Free Disclosures*. If *ex ante* policies are likely to result in depressed or zero patent royalties, then one might expect to see more disclosures of royalty-free (RF) licensing terms at SDOs adopting such policies than at SDOs not adopting such policies. Interestingly, our data reveal the opposite effect. As shown in Table G.1 below, from 2007 to 2010, at VITA there was only one *ex ante* disclosure of royalty-free licensing terms (14% of all disclosures), while at IEEE there were 11 (84%) and at IETF there were 283 (100%).

Table G.1
Royalty-Related Disclosures (2007-2010)

	VITA	IEEE	IETF
Standards Approved	18	333	1,243
Total Patent Disclosures	7	349	481
Standards Covered by Disclosures	7	103	594
Royalty-Free/Non-Assert (RF) Disclosures	1	11	283
Non-Zero Royalty Disclosures	6	2	0

The royalty-free disclosures made at IEEE and IETF were not mandated by a formal SDO policy, and there are various other explanations for the prevalence of royalty-free licensing, particularly in view of stated preferences at IETF.[138] Likewise, VITA's *ex ante* requirement to disclose maximum royalty rates does not appear to have subjected patent holders to inordinate pressure to license their patents for too little, or for free. If such pressure existed, then even if a patent holder initially disclosed a reasonable royalty rate, one might expect it subsequently to revise its royalty disclosure to reflect a lower rate more to the liking of implementers. At VITA, however, we have identified only one instance in which a disagreement over licensing terms initiated after an *ex ante* disclosure resulted in the amendment of the license disclosure made by the patent holder. Interestingly, that disagreement involved not royalties, but the scope of a "defensive suspension" provision.[139] Thus, there have to date been no downward adjustments to royalty rates disclosed under the VITA *ex ante* policy.

---

[137] *See, e.g.*, 2007 DOJ/FTC Report, *supra* note 14, at 52; Herman, *supra* note 11, at 38 ("through coordinated action, the prospective licensees will pressure the patentee to forgo royalties or fees altogether").

[138] *See* IETF RFC 3979, *supra* note 74, at §8 ("In general, IETF working groups prefer technologies with no known IPR claims or, for technologies with claims against them, an offer of royalty-free licensing.")

[139] A "defensive suspension" clause allows the patent holder to suspend or terminate a license grant if the licensee takes some specified action, typically bringing suit against the licensor. *See* ABA Manual, *supra*

Admittedly, the maximum royalty rates disclosed under an SDO's *ex ante* policy are not necessarily indicative of the *actual* royalty rates agreed by patent holders and implementers in bilateral license agreements. Moreover, we have no way to determine whether the initial royalty rates disclosed by patent holders under VITA's *ex ante* policy are justified or artificially depressed due to pressure from implementers. Thus, while the data noted above do not point to inappropriate pressure to depress patent royalty rates, they do not shed light on whether or not such royalty reductions occurred in fact.

2. *Survey Responses re. Royalty Disclosures.* We asked VITA members what actions they took in response to *ex ante* royalty disclosures when they felt that the disclosed royalty was "too high". 33% (n=13) of respondents felt that, at on at least one occasion, a royalty rate disclosed at VITA was too high. The actions taken by these respondents as a result of such disclosures are summarized in Table G.2 below.

Table G.2
VITA Participant Actions When Disclosed Royalty "Too High"

Response	n=
Raised issue at meeting	3
Attempted to design around patent	2
Delayed/stopped development pending resolution	3
Contacted/negotiated with patent holder	2
Voted against approval of proposed standard	1

Unlike most of our survey questions, this one was open-ended in that respondents were asked to compose an answer without selecting from a list of pre-determined choices. We believe it is significant that, given this flexibility, only one respondent explicitly stated that he or she had attempted to negotiate the royalty rate with the patent holder. One other respondent who stated that he/she had "contacted" the patent holder can also be assumed to have done so in order to negotiate a royalty rate. Bilateral discussions of royalty rates are normal in the standards development context and are, in fact, encouraged by critics of *ex ante* policies as the optimal method of setting royalty rates.[140] Other responses, such as attempting to design around the patent or postponing further

---

note 8, at 62-67. Lindsay describes the episode as follows based on a 2009 interview with VITA's executive director:

> "The company had included what other members of the group evidently considered an overly broad "defensive termination" provision. After reading the provision, representatives of those other member companies discussed the issue with the patent-holder. When that did not resolve the difference, the member companies filed formal complaints with VITA, saying the provisions were neither fair nor reasonable. VITA and its counsel discussed the matter with the patent-holder, who reconsidered its position and removed the clause."

Lindsay, *supra* note 24, at 8.

[140] *See* Herman, *supra* note 11, at 39.

development pending resolution of the issue, might at best put indirect pressure on the patent holder to lower its royalty offer, though this form of pressure is simply the sort of cost-based competition that was encouraged by the DOJ when it analyzed the VITA and IEEE *ex ante* policies.[141] Thus, while there are inherent limitations on survey data in this context (i.e., few participants would likely admit that they engaged in unlawful collusion to pressure patent holders to depress royalties), it is informative that the VITA participants who responded to this question reported taking a range of appropriate and lawful actions in response to *ex ante* royalty disclosures that they felt were excessive.

        3.   *Conclusion.* Some of the data we analyzed suggests that *ex ante* policies have not led to a depression of royalty rates, and we found no evidence that affirmatively supports such a causal association. However, due to inherent limitations of the royalty data available to us, this result remains inconclusive and a desirable subject for further research.

---

[141] *See* 2007 DOJ/FTC Report, *supra* note 14, at 52-53 ("*Ex ante* licensing discussions may lead to price competition, in effect allowing for broader competition among alternative technologies vying for inclusion in the standard... *Ex ante* licensing discussions can thus preserve the benefits of competition that exist by increasing the *ex ante* knowledge of SSO decision-makers about licensing terms and may improve the quality of their decisions, enabling them to make tradeoffs between price and technical merit...").

V. Conclusions

A. *Summary of Findings.*

As described above, we reviewed a variety of empirical data within the framework of six predictions made by critics of *ex ante* licensing disclosure policies. These predictions, and our observations, are briefly summarized below:

1. **Assertion**: *Ex ante* policies will reduce standardization activity.

   Observation: We observed *increases* in both new standards activity and standards approved at both VITA and IEEE following adoption of their *ex ante* policies.

2. **Assertion**: *Ex ante* policies will cause standards to take longer to develop.

   Observation: Standardization time measurably decreased at IEEE following adoption of its *ex ante* policy. Standardization time at VITA increased, but at a slower rate than prior to policy adoption, and in a manner consistent with broader industry behavior exemplified by IETF. Perceptions among a significant number of VITA standards developers, particularly those having greater experience with the organization, was that standardization time had either decreased or remained constant following adoption of the *ex ante* policy.

3. **Assertion**: *Ex ante* policies will require standards developers to devote more time to standardization activities.

   Observation: Among VITA participants having greater experience with the organization or SDOs in general, and among participants who checked for *ex ante* licensing disclosures, there was a general sense that the adoption of VITA's *ex ante* policy did not result in an increased individual time commitment.

4. **Assertion**: *Ex ante* policies will cause members to withdraw from SDOs that adopt them.

   Observation: Overall VITA membership has increased since the adoption of its *ex ante* policy in 2007, despite material year-to-year fluctuations in membership. We did not find evidence suggesting that more than one VITA member resigned from the organization as a result of the adoption of VITA's *ex ante* policy.

5. **Assertion**: *Ex ante* policies will cause standards to decrease in quality.

Observation: We did not find evidence that the quality of VITA standards deteriorated following adoption of its *ex ante* policy, and found some evidence suggesting that quality improved.

6.   **Assertion**: *Ex ante* policies will depress patent royalty rates.

Observations: We found no evidence that affirmatively supports such an association. However, due to inherent limitations of the royalty data available to us, this result remains inconclusive and a desirable subject for further research.

B.   *Limitations and Generalizability of Findings*.

Many of the findings in this study are based on analyses of data supplied by VITA, a relatively small organization. It has been suggested in the literature that VITA's positive experience with *ex ante* licensing disclosures has been atypical, and that the perceived benefits of *ex ante* disclosures to VITA might not translate to larger SDOs with greater numbers of standards, patents and participants.[142] While we also analyzed publicly-available data from IEEE, a much larger SDO, our ability to obtain information from IEEE was limited and IEEE declined our request to permit us to survey its members. Thus, our analysis of IEEE was not as complete as our analysis of VITA. Moreover, our analysis of survey responses by VITA participants was limited by the survey response rate (53.4%) and margin of error (9.8%). In year-to-year comparisons of data relating to standards starts, standards approved and membership levels, time-varying factors that were not observed may have had a significant effect, and relationships between the variables studied may have been distorted by confounding factors that we were not able to control for.

Despite these limitations, we believe that the analyses and conclusions in this study are generalizable to other standardization activities in the ICT industry. First, VITA's membership ranges from large, multi-national corporations with significant patent portfolios to small businesses.[143] Thus, while VITA's overall membership may be smaller than that of other SDOs, we believe that it is generally representative of the range of businesses that participate in ICT standardization. Second, as shown by the data in Tables A.1, B.1, B.2 and C.1, VITA's standardization projects, while fewer in number than those conducted at IEEE and IETF, share many characteristics with projects conducted at these larger organizations. In particular, the ratio of patent disclosures filed to approved standards at VITA, IEEE and IETF are comparable. Thus, the fact that VITA may approve five standards in a year rather than 50 or 500 does not necessarily imply that the five standards activities at VITA differ materially in scope, complexity, patent coverage or value from any five given standards activities conducted at larger SDOs. For these reasons, we believe that the conclusions drawn based on data collected

---

[142] *See* TAPIA, *supra* note 24, at 178-79 (describing the reasoning of *ex ante* critics who sought to differentiate VITA from larger, more complex organizations such as ETSI).
[143] *See* note 126, *supra*.

from VITA has applicability to other standardization activities in the ICT sector and should inform the discussion of *ex ante* disclosure policies in general.

C. *Conclusion*

In general, we did not find that *ex ante* disclosure policies resulted in measurable negative effects on the number of standards started or adopted, personal time commitments or quality of standards, nor was there compelling evidence that *ex ante* policies caused the lengthening of time required for standardization or the depression of royalty rates. There was also evidence to suggest that the adoption of *ex ante* policies may have contributed to positive effects observed on some of these variables. In addition, a significant majority of VITA participants responding to our survey felt that the information elicited by the organization's *ex ante* policy was important and improved the overall openness and transparency of the standards-development process. Thus, while there are numerous areas in which further study and analysis may be warranted, and other organizations in which the implementation of *ex ante* policies may have different effects, we conclude, on the basis of the data that we have reviewed, that the process-based criticisms of *ex ante* policies described above, and the predicted negative effects flowing from the adoption of such polices, are not supported by the evidence reviewed.

DATA APPENDICES

A.   Demographic Characteristics of VITA Survey Respondents

Table S.A.1
Industry Sector

Sector	Percentage (n=44)
Vendor	74%
Customer (including government customers)	19%
Government (regulatory)	2%
Other	4%

Table S.A.2
Job Function

Job Function	Percentage (n=45)
Engineering	57%
Business/Management	26%
Marketing	13%
Legal	0%

Table S.A.3
SDO Experience

Actively Participates in How Many SDOs	Percentage (n=47)
1-2	62%
3-5	23%
More than 5	15%

Table S.A.4
Tenure with VITA

Number of Years of Participation in VITA	Percentage (n=45)
Less than 1	23%
1-2	26%
3-5	17%
5-9	11%
10 or more	23%

Table S.A.5
Patent Experience

Listed as Inventor on How Many Patents?	Percentage (n=47)
None	57%
1-5	32%
More than 5	11%

B.   Ex Ante Disclosures

Table S.B.1
Ex Ante Disclosures at VITA (2007-2010)

Disclosure	# Patents† Disclosed	Standards Covered	Std. Approved	Royalty Structure§
1	9	2	Yes	Fixed fee + per unit royalty
2	1	1	No	Fixed fee + per unit royalty
3*	1	1**	No	Fixed fee + per unit royalty
4	1	1	Yes	Fixed fee
5	1	1	Yes	Per unit royalty
6*	3	1	No	Royalty-free
7	5	1	No	Fixed fee + per unit royalty

* Company previously making disclosure
**Same standard as Disclosure #2
† Includes patent applications
§ Researchers have agreed not to disclose specific royalty rates or companies making disclosures, per agreement with VITA.

C.   Time to Standardization

Table S.C.1
Average Time (in days) for Standards Approval (2003-2010)

Year	VITA	IEEE	IETF
2003	1174	1342	694
2004	n/a	1551	730
2005	379	1578	848
2006	1383	1630	873
2007	1138	1625	893
2008	1542	1387	966
2009	1275	1529	954
2010	1235	1449	925

D. **Standards Activity**

Table S.D.1
Number of New Standards Activities Started, by Year

Year	VITA	IEEE	IETF
2004	16	87	1085
2005	12	78	1431
2006	5	83	1434
2007	7	100	1298
2008	19	120	1201
2009	5	145	1353
2010	10	187	1533

Table S.D.2
Number of Standards Approved, by Year

Year	VITA	IEEE	IETF
2003	5	61	262
2004	0	84	327
2005	2	78	343
2006	2	76	332
2007	2	77	311
2008	3	77	285
2009	5	78	306
2010	8	84	341

SELECTED REFERENCES

Cases

In re. Dell Computer Corp., 121 F.T.C. 616 (1996)

Rambus, Inc. v. Infineon Technologies AG, 318 F.3d 1081 (Fed. Cir. 2003), cert. denied, 124 S.Ct. 227 (2003)

Decision and Order, *In the Matter of Negotiated Data Solutions LLC* (FTC, Sept. 9, 2008), FTC File No. 051-0094

Regulatory and Agency Materials

Deborah Platt Majoras, *Recognizing the Procompetitive Potential of Royalty Discussions in Standard Setting*, Remarks prepared for "Standardization and the Law: Developing the Golden Mean for Global Trade", Stanford Law School, Sept. 23, 2005.

U.S. Dept. of Justice, *Business Review Letter to VMEbus International Trade Association (VITA)* (Oct. 30, 2006)

U.S. Dept. of Justice, *Business Review Letter to Institute of Electrical and Electronics Engineers (IEEE)* (Apr. 30, 2007)

U.S. Dept. of Justice & U.S. Fed. Trade Comm., ANTITRUST ENFORCEMENT AND INTELLECTUAL PROPERTY RIGHTS: PROMOTING INNOVATION AND COMPETITION 42-48 (2007)

U.S. Federal Trade Commission, THE EVOLVING IP MARKETPLACE: ALIGNING PATENT NOTICE AND REMEDIES WITH COMPETITION (2011)

European Commission, GUIDELINES ON THE APPLICABILITY OF ARTICLE 101 OF THE TREATY ON THE FUNCTIONING OF THE EUROPEAN UNION TO HORIZONTAL CO-OPERATION AGREEMENTS (2011)

Books and Articles

AMERICAN BAR ASSOCIATION, COMMITTEE ON TECHNICAL STANDARDIZATION, SECTION OF SCIENCE & TECHNOLOGY LAW, STANDARDS DEVELOPMENT PATENT POLICY MANUAL (Jorge L. Contreras, ed., 2007)

Rudi Bekkers & Joel West, *IPR Standardization Policies and Strategic Patenting in UMTS* (presented at 25th Celebration Conference 2008 on Entrepreneurship and Innovation – Organizations, Institutions, Systems and Regions)

Pierre-André Dubois, *Standardization, FRAND Terms and Patent Misuse – Recent Developments*, EUROPEAN ANTITRUST REV. 2007 at 68

Maurits Dolmans, *Standards for Standards*, 26 FORDHAM INTL. L.J. 163 (2002)

Einer Elhauge, *Do Patent Holdup and Royalty Stacking Lead to Systematically Excessive Royalties?*, 4 J. COMPETITION L. & ECON. 535 (2008)

Joseph Farrell, *Choosing the Rules for Formal Standardization* (working paper, U.C. Berkeley, Dept. Economics 1996) (available at http://citeseerx.ist.psu.edu/viewdoc/download?doi=10.1.1.73.6537&rep=rep1&type=pdf)

A. Michael Froomkin, *Habermas@Discourse.net: Toward a Critical Theory of Cyberspace*, 116 HARV. L. REV. 749, 783 (2003)

Damien Geradin, Anne Layne-Farrar, & A. Jorge Padilla, *The Ex Ante Auction Model for the Control of Market Power in Standard Setting Organizations* (working paper, Apr. 2007) (available at SSRN: http://ssrn.com/abstract=979393)

Letter from Michele Herman, Davis Wright Tremaine LLP to Patrick Gallagher, National Institute of Standards and Technology, March 4, 2011 (available at http://standards.gov/standards_gov/sos_rfi_docs/26_Herman_DWTLLP.pdf)

Michele K. Herman, *How the Deal is Done, Part 1*, LANDSLIDE, Sept/Oct 2010, at 35

Michele Herman, *The Quandary of a Balanced IPR Policy*, LICENSING J., Oct. 2006, at 5

Intellectual Property Owners Association, Standards Primer – An Overview of the Standards Setting Bodies and Patent-Related Issues That Arise in the Context of Standards-Setting Activities (Sept. 2009) (available at http://www.ipo.org/AM/Template.cfm?Section=Patents&Template=/MembersOnly.cfm&NavMenuID=1454&ContentID=24139&DirectListComboInd=D).

Anne Layne-Farrar, Gerard Llobet & A. Jorge Padilla, *Preventing Patent Hold up: An Economic Assessment of Ex Ante Licensing Negotiations in Standard Setting* (working paper, May 2008) (available at SSRN: http://ssrn.com/abstract=1129551)

Anne Layne-Farrar, A. Jorge Padilla & Richard Schmalensee, *Pricing Patents for Licensing in Standard-Setting Organizations: Making Sense of FRAND Commitments*, 74 ANTITRUST L.J. 671 (2007).

Mark A. Lemley, *Ten Things to do About Patent Holdup of Standards (and One Not To)*, 48 BOSTON COLL. L. REV. 149 (2007)

Mark A. Lemley, *Intellectual Property Rights and Standard-Setting Organizations*, 90 CAL. L. REV. 1889 (2002)

Mark Lemley & Carl Shapiro, *Patent Holdup and Royalty Stacking*, 85 TEX. L. REV. 1991 (2007).

Michael A. Lindsay, *Negotiating Royalty or Other License Terms Before the Standard is Set* (presented at Am. Intell. Prop. L. Assn. 2009 Spring Meeting) (available at http://www.dorsey.com/files/upload/lindsay_negotiating_royalties_AIPLA_spring09.pdf)

Gil Ohana, Marc Hansen & Omar Shah, *Disclosure and Negotiation of Licensing Terms Prior to Adoption of Industry Standards: Preventing Another Patent Ambush?* [2003] EUROPEAN COMPETITION L. REV. 644 (2003)

M. Sean Royall, Amanda Tessar & Aaron Di Vincenzo, *Deterring "Patent Ambush" in Standard Setting: Lessons Learned from Rambus and Qualcomm*, ANTITRUST, Summer 2009 at 34

Marc Rysman & Tim Simcoe, *A NAASTy Alternative to RAND Pricing Commitments* (working paper 2011) (available at http://people.bu.edu/tsimcoe/documents/published/NAAST.pdf)

Marc Rysman & Tim Simcoe, *Patents and the Performance of Voluntary Standard Setting Organizations*, 54 MANAGEMENT SCI. 1920 (2008)

Rajiv C. Shah & Jay P. Kesan, *Open Standards and the Role of Politics*, PROC. 8TH ANN. INTL. DIGITAL GOVT. RESEARCH CONF. (2007)

Rajiv C. Shah & Jay P. Kesan, *An Empirical Examination of Open Standards Development* (U. Ill L. & Econ. Research Papers Series, Research Paper No. LE07-039) (2007) (available at http://papers.ssrn.com/sol3/papers.cfm?abstract_id=1031749)

CARL SHAPIRO & HAL R. VARIAN, INFORMATION RULES: A STRATEGIC GUIDE TO THE NETWORK ECONOMY 238-42 (1999)

Robert A. Skitol, *Concerted Buying Power: Its Potential For Addressing The Patent Holdup Problem in Standard Setting*, 72 ANTITRUST L.J. 727 (2005)

Robert A. Skitol & Kenneth M. Vorrasi, *Patent Holdup in Standards Development: Life After Rambus v. FTC*, ANTITRUST, Spring 2009 at 26

Tim Simcoe, *Delay and de jure Standardization: Exploring the Slowdown in Internet Standards Development* in STANDARDS AND PUBLIC POLICY 260 (2006)

Daniel G. Swanson & William J. Baumol, *Reasonable and Nondiscriminatory (RAND) Royalties, Standards Selection, and Control of Market Power*, 73 ANTITRUST L.J. 1 (2005)

Richard S. Taffet, *Ex Ante Licensing in Standards Development – Myths and Reality* (presented to AIPLA Spring Meeting, May 4, 2006) (available at http://www.bingham.com/Media.aspx?MediaID=2742)

CLAUDIA TAPIA, INDUSTRIAL PROPERTY RIGHTS, TECHNICAL STANDARDS AND LICENSING PRACTICES (FRAND) IN THE TELECOMMUNICATIONS INDUSTRY (2010)

Andrew Updegrove, *Ex Ante Disclosure: Risks, Rewards, Process and Alternatives*, CONSORTIUM STANDARDS BUL., June 2006, at 1

HAL R. VARIAN, JOSEPH FARRELL & CARL SHAPIRO, THE ECONOMICS OF INFORMATION TECHNOLOGY – AN INTRODUCTION (2004)

Tor Winston, *Innovation and Ex Ante Consideration of Licensing Terms in Standard Setting*, U.S. Dept. Justice Economic Analysis Group Discussion Paper EAG 06-3 (Mar. 2006) (available at http://www.justice.gov/atr/public/eag/221875.pdf)